NEW PERSPECTIVES ON ORGANIZATION THEORY

Contributions in Sociology
SERIES EDITOR: DON MARTINDALE
University of Minnesota

1. NEW PERSPECTIVES ON ORGANIZATION THEORY:
An Empirical Reconsideration
of the Marxian and Classical Analyses
William L. Zwerman

2. GARRISON COMMUNITY:
A Study of an Overseas American Military Colony
Charlotte Wolf

3. SMALL TOWN AND THE NATION:
The Conflict of Local and Translocal Forces
Don Martindale and R. Galen Hanson

contributions in sociology 1

William L. Zwerman

NEW PERSPECTIVES ON ORGANIZATION THEORY

AN EMPIRICAL RECONSIDERATION OF
THE MARXIAN AND CLASSICAL ANALYSES

Greenwood Publishing Corporation

Westport, Connecticut

Copyright © 1970 by William L. Zwerman
All rights reserved. No portion of this book may be
reproduced, by any process or technique, without the
express written consent of the author and publisher.
Library of Congress Catalog Card Number: 71-90791
SBN: 8371-1851-4
Greenwood Publishing Corporation
51 Riverside Avenue, Westport, Conn. 06880
Greenwood Publishers, Ltd., 42 Hanway Street, London, W.1., England
Printed in the United States of America
Designed by Joan Stoliar

To Sara and Paul

CONTENTS

PREFACE	xv
ACKNOWLEDGMENTS	xix

1 THE MARXIAN AND CLASSICAL ANALYSES OF TECHNOLOGY, INDUSTRIAL ORGANIZATION, AND PRODUCTION — 1

2 THE ORGANIZATIONAL CHARACTERISTICS OF ENGLISH AND MIDWESTERN AMERICAN INDUSTRIES — 26

3 TYPES OF MANAGEMENT SYSTEMS — 45

4 ORGANIZATIONAL STRUCTURE — 60

5 TECHNOLOGY AND LABOR — 95

THE SOCIAL MILIEU **6** 124

THE CONFRONTATION OF
MARXIAN AND CLASSICAL
THEORIES OF ORGANIZATION **7** 141

APPENDIXES 161
BIBLIOGRAPHY 205
INDEX 213

TABLES

1 Production Technology and Level of Business Success in Minneapolis and Essex Firms   32

2 Size of Labor Force and Level of Business Success in Minneapolis Firms   33

3 Separation of Ownership and Management and Level of Business Success in Minneapolis Firms   35

4 Separation of Ownership and Management and Type of Management System in Minneapolis Firms   50

5 Size of Labor Force and Type of Management System in Minneapolis Firms   51

6 Production Technology and Type of Management System in Minneapolis Firms   53

7 Production Technology, Size of Labor Force, and Type of Management System in Minneapolis Firms   55

8 Production Technology, Span of Control of Chief Executive, and Level of Business Success in Minneapolis and English Firms   67

9 Production Technology, Ratio of Nonsupervisory to Supervisory Personnel, and Level of Business Success in Minneapolis and English Firms   71

10 Production Technology, Number of Levels of Management, and Level of Business Success in Minneapolis and English Firms   73

11 Size of Labor Force, Span of Control of Chief Executive, and Level of Business Success in Minneapolis Firms   77

12 Size of Labor Force, Number of Levels of Management, and Level of Business Success in Mineapolis Firms   79

13 Separation of Ownership and Management, Span of Control of Chief Executive, and Level of Business Success in Minneapolis Firms   83

14 Separation of Ownership and Management, Number of Levels of Management, and Level of Business Success in Minneapolis Firms   85

15 Production Technology, Ratio of Production to Nonproduction Workers, and Level of Business Success in Minneapolis and Essex Firms   100

16 Production Technology, Ratio of Supervisors to Managers, and Level of Business Success in Minneapolis Firms   103

17 Production Technology, Level of Business Success, and Promotion Policy in Minneapolis Firms   106

18 Production Technology, Level of Business Success, and Labor Costs in Minneapolis and Essex Firms   108

19 Separation of Ownership and Management, Ratio of Production to Nonproduction Workers, and Level of Business Success in Minneapolis Firms   113

20 Ratio of Supervisors to Managers by Ownership Type and Level of Business Success in Minneapolis Firms   116

21 Separation of Ownership and Management, Promotion Policy, and Level of Business Success in Minneapolis Firms   117

22 Separation of Ownership and Management, Labor Costs, and Level of Business Success in Minneapolis Firms   119

23 Production Technology and Organizational Dependence on Local Markets for Production Materials in Minneapolis Firms   129

24 Size of Labor Force and Dependence upon Local Markets for Production Materials in Minneapolis Firms   131

25 Production Technology, Size of Labor Force, and Dependence upon Local Markets for Production Materials in Minneapolis Firms   133

26 Production Technology, Level of Business Success, and Organizational Dependence on Local Markets for Sales in Minneapolis Firms   135

27 Size of Labor Force, Level of Business Success, and Organizational Dependence on Local Markets for Sales in Minneapolis Firms 136

28 Production Technology, Size of Labor Force, and Organizational Dependence on Local Markets for Sales in Minneapolis Firms 137

29 Distribution of Production Technologies in Minneapolis and Essex Samples 172

30 Production Technology, Size of Labor Force, and Level of Business Success in Minneapolis Firms 173

31 Separation of Ownership and Management, and Level of Business Success in Smaller Minneapolis Firms 174

32 Type of Management System and Level of Business Success in Minneapolis Firms 174

33 Number of Levels of Management Hierarchy and Level of Business Success in Minneapolis Firms 175

34 Span of Control of Chief Executive and Level of Business Success in Minneapolis Firms 176

35 Span of Control of First-Line Supervisor and Level of Business Success in Minneapolis Firms 177

36 Ratio of Nonsupervisory Personnel to Supervisors and Level of Business Success in Minneapolis Firms 178

37 Ratio of Production to Nonproduction Workers and Level of Business Success in Minneapolis Firms   179

38 Ratio of Nonmanagerial Supervisors to Managers and Level of Business Success in Minneapolis Firms   180

39 Labor Costs and Level of Business Success in Minneapolis Firms   181

40 Promotion Policy and Level of Business Success in Minneapolis Firms   181

41 Dependence upon Local Markets for Production Supplies and Level of Business Success in Minneapolis Firms   182

42 Dependence upon Local Markets for Sales and Level of Business Success in Minneapolis Firms   182

43 Production Technology, Span of Control of First-Line Supervisors, and Level of Business Success in Minneapolis Firms   184

44 Size of Labor Force, Span of Control of First-Line Supervisors, and Level of Business Success in Minneapolis Firms   185

45 Size of Labor Force, Ratio of Nonsupervisory to Supervisory Personnel, and Level of Business Success in Minneapolis Firms   186

46 Separation of Ownership and Management, Span of Control of First-Line Supervisors, and Level of Business Success in Minneapolis Firms   188

47 Separation of Ownership and Management, Ratio of Nonsupervisory to Supervisory Personnel, and Level of Business Success in Minneapolis Firms   189

48 Size of Labor Force, Ratio of Production to Nonproduction Workers, and Level of Business Success in Minneapolis Firms   192

49 Size of Labor Force, Ratio of Supervisors to Managers, and Level of Business Success in Minneapolis Firms   193

50 Size of Labor Force, Promotion Policy, and Level of Business Success in Minneapolis Firms   194

51 Separation of Ownership and Management, Dependence upon Local Markets for Production Supplies, and Level of Business Success in Minneapolis Firms   196

52 Separation of Ownership and Management, Dependence upon Local Markets for Sales, and Level of Business Success in Minneapolis Firms   197

PREFACE

It may very well be that the ghost of Marx has hovered over sociological theory during its development in the twentieth century but the substance of his work has often been very difficult to locate.[1]

The absence of the Marxian perspective has been particularly noticeable in the analysis of formal organizations, despite the fact that Marx was vitally concerned with the structure, operation, and interrelations of this form of organization, especially in the economic and political sectors of the society. In point of fact the sociological analysis of formal organizations has been shaped by two broad conservative perspectives.

The first dominant perspective has been business management theory, including classical management theory, human relations, and decisional theory. These viewpoints are closely tied to classical economics and explicitly anti-Marxian. The second general perspective has been functional analysis, a point of view which is extremely conservative in concept, if not intent. One of the results of this conservative domination has been an omission of consideration of such core Marxian concepts as material determinism, conflict, and exploitation.

In 1958 Joan Woodward began publishing the results of a research project designed to test some of the key assumptions and hypotheses contained in the classical analysis of formal organizations, specifically manufacturing organizations. Out of this analysis, conducted in the southeast Essex area of England, came a set of findings which thrust the role of technology into a position it had not previously enjoyed in the tradition of formal organization analysis. This research, further, brought several of the major tenets of the classical tradition under severe attack.[2]

The present study is a modified replication, in an American setting, of Woodward's pioneering work. The analysis which follows attempts to reconstruct Woodward's analysis, to provide the beginning of a theoretical perspective which allows for the inclusion of concepts central to both the classical and Marxian traditions, and to suggest empirical and conceptual extensions of her work.

The theoretical focus here is on two great ideological

traditions of the western world. The rise to dominance of complex formal organizations in the nineteenth and twentieth centuries has been viewed ambivalently by conservatives and radicals alike. Today even liberalism, the ideological carrier of this form of organization, has come to question these institutions, particularly as they appear to affect the quality of contemporary social life. The social centrality of this form of organization, the universal ambivalence manifested toward it, and the ideological overtones of the perspectives utilized in its analysis combine to make it only natural that the analysis of formal organizations should include a perspective which focuses explicitly upon ideology. Ideology has not only rationalized the modern world but it has often dominated the analysis of the organizational form which today dominates this world.

This analysis parallels Woodward's in emphasizing the impact of production technology on industrial organization. Its results, however, differ sufficiently to raise some interesting questions about the influence of the general socioeconomic milieu on the organization of these firms. One of the more interesting differences observed between English and American firms is that the United States firms appear top-heavy by English standards, having considerably more supervisory personnel. The interpretation advanced in this study views this as a function of American affluence, a condition which allows for greater arbitrary disbursement of material and status rewards within the firm. In this connection it is interesting to note that one of the perennial "Fortune 100" has been experiencing financial difficulty and this winter announced the reduction of its corporate staff from 1,510 to 132. It thus seems that it is not only possible but necessary to combine classical market-milieu variables with Marxian considerations of the material basis of industrial organizations in the analysis of these organizational forms.

Students working in empirical disciplines cannot afford the luxury of substituting rationalization and social strategies in the place of description and explanation.

William L. Zwerman
Minneapolis
April, 1969

NOTES

1. Irving Zeitlin, *Ideology and the Development of Sociological Theory* (Englewood Cliffs, N.J.: Prentice-Hall, 1968).

2. Joan Woodward, *Management and Technology,* Problems of Progress in Industry, No. 3 (London: Her Majesty's Stationery Office, Department of Scientific and Industrial Research, 1958); idem, *Industrial Organization: Theory and Practice* (London: Oxford University Press, 1965).

ACKNOWLEDGMENTS

I would like to express a special indebtedness to three persons for their assistance and encouragement in the completion of this study.

Throughout this work Don Martindale functioned simultaneously as a friend, colleague, and teacher. He was always present when needed and provided a kind of personal support that was absolutely vital to me. His knowledge and insight was a constant source of amazement. If I "fly" at all in this analysis it is because of him.

Robert Dubin followed this work from start to finish and provided invaluable personal and intellectual aid. If I "fly" too far, it will never be his fault; he constantly struggled to inform me of the relationship between data and interpretation.

The aid of my wife, Patricia Stewart Zwerman, was of inestimable importance. The debt to her is total and considerably greater than any which are more specific.

1

THE MARXIAN AND CLASSICAL ANALYSES OF TECHNOLOGY, INDUSTRIAL ORGANIZATION, AND PRODUCTION

In the field of formal organizational analysis there is a broad difference of opinion among Marxians and non-Marxians as to the relationship between technology and formal organization. This difference is most clearly manifested in the analysis of industrial organizations, where the Marxians presuppose the primacy of industrial technology, treating social relations (in the first instance the individual organization itself) as secondary, i.e., superstructures. Non-Marxian social scientists, while paying lip service to technology, place primary stress on the structure of the organized enterprise, in line with the classical point of view.

A recent study of English industry has dramatically revealed the presence of these divergent tendencies and has forced a reconsideration of both traditions.[1]

Historically, formal organizations have been viewed by the classicists as products of the extension of human rationality—an extension that includes the technology of the organization—and social systems relying on consensus and cooperation for their proper functioning. The Marxians, on the other hand, saw formal organizations as social units which in noncommunist nations were manipulated by capitalists in their never-ending conflict with workers—the primary focus of their manipulation being on economic and technological variables.

In the analysis of formal organizations, then, the critical elements of these divergent positions are the evaluations of the relationship between the material aspects of the organizations—economy and technology—and their social relations together with the cooperation-conflict element in these social units. In the development of that part of organizational theory *focusing on formal organizations,* explicit concern with the relationship between the material and nonmaterial and with conflict has come late to the field.

Well into the 1960s the *dominant* perspectives in the analysis of formal organizations were classical management and human-relations theory. Both of these traditions conceived of the organization as an extension of man's rationality, part of a search for greater productive effectiveness and efficiency, and as social contexts where cooperation among members of the organization would produce the greatest good for the greatest number. Technology was looked upon as a tool in the service of these ends and conflict as an illness that could be cured through the proper manipulation of the relationships involving the members of the organization.[2]

In this respect the dominant traditions in the field were completely consistent with their origins in classical economic theory, which accepted the liberal idea of progress wherein development of these organizations provided for the general welfare and in which technology, in the words of Alfred Marshall, was but "a mere implement of production."

A stark contrast to this position is presented in Marx's writing on the unending conflict between capitalists and workers, his theory of exploitation, and his evaluation of the role of technology in the context of formal organizations, particularly the industrial organizations which were developing rapidly in the England of his day.

> These two descriptions are far from being identical. In one, the collective labourer, or social body of labour, appears as the dominant subject and the mechanical automaton as the object; in the other, the automaton itself is the subject, and the workmen are merely conscious organs, coordinate with the unconscious organs of the automaton, and together with them, subordinated to the central moving-power. The first description is applicable to every possible employment of machinery on a large scale, the second is characteristic of its use by capital, and therefore of the modern factory system. Ure prefers therefore, to describe the central machine, from which the motion comes, not

only as an automaton, but as an autocrat. "In these spacious halls the benignant power of steam summons around him his myriads of willing menials."³

Here as everywhere else, we must distinguish between the increased productiveness due to the development of the social process of production, and that due to the capitalist exploitation of that process.⁴

The technical subordination of the workman to the uniform motion of the instruments of labour, and the peculiar composition of the body of workpeople, consisting as it does of individuals of both sexes and all ages, give rise to a barrack discipline, which is elaborated into a complete system in the factory, and which fully develops the before mentioned labour of overlooking, thereby dividing the workpeople into operatives and overlookers, into private soldiers and sergeants of an industrial army.⁵

Occasionally the Marxian conception of the relationship between technology and formal organization would appear momentarily in the literature on formal organization, such as in the work of Chinoy and of Walker and Guest.⁶ But the idea that organizational technology might be a major category of independent variables in the analysis of formal organizations was largely ignored. Indeed, it was probably more often the case that suggestions to include the Marxian perspective on the relationship between technology and formal organization were viewed, in the words of Alvin Gouldner, as an "atavistic recurrence of technological determinism."⁷

It is obviously time to reconsider the relationships between the major variables contained in the classical and radical traditions in the context of the analysis of formal organizations.

TECHNOLOGY AND FORMAL ORGANIZATIONS

Although the general impact of technology on social and cultural patterns is widely recognized, its impact on formal organization has not received much attention. The lack of attention devoted to this area is amply documented by the dearth of studies of the man-machine relationship disclosed by Martin Meissner in a 1964 Ph.D. dissertation. In preparing his dissertation Meissner was able to locate only thirty-five case studies dealing with the relationship between formal organization and technology, and only twenty-three of these were in English. Further documentation of this neglect is provided by Thompson's search of the literature for typologies of technologies, which yielded the contribution of Joan Woodward together with one unpublished typology of psychiatric treatment technologies.[8] This lack of concern with the links between technology[9] and specific organizational forms is rooted in assumptions current in the social sciences—assumptions expressed by Wilbur Moore in a 1965 publication. Moore maintains the social characteristics of industry are best viewed as conditions and consequences of its technical characteristics. This would seem to place technology in the forefront of analysis, but Moore quickly adds that the social organization of industry is in fact only partly a correlate or derivative of technology.[10] There is no question that Moore's way of putting the matter reflects the consensus. However, in practice this opinion has worked to direct attention away from the influence of technology. Formal organization is viewed by the majority of students as the product of human decisions in which technology is only a set of limiting conditions.

The widely held notion of the incidental role of technology in formal organization is seriously challenged by the findings of an English study, conducted in the mid-1950s and published in 1958. In a series of case studies, variations in the organizational characteristics of firms were nearly always found to be linked to differences in techniques of production. Thus it was possible to infer a cause-and-effect relationship between a system of production and its associated organizational pattern.[11]

The English study of the relationship between organization and technology in industrial manufacturing firms reported in 1958 was followed by a more comprehensive analysis in 1965.[12] The conclusions of the first report were further documented in the second, and considerably more data were presented to substantiate the argument that technology and social organization are related in a cause-and-effect fashion.

NATURE OF THE WOODWARD STUDY

The mid-1950s analysis conducted by a team of researchers from the South East Essex Technical College examined 100 manufacturing firms in the area, almost all the firms having a labor force of 100 or greater.

In both reports on the South Essex studies Joan Woodward presented evidence of direct ties between technology and organization. She theorized that different types of production technologies require different patterns of organization for optimal operating effectiveness. There is no single optimal form of organization for all types of industrial firms —rather a set of optimal types of organization specific to particular types of technology.

Woodward's analysis utilizes four sets of variables: two concern the technology of the organization; the third consists of social characteristics of the organization, and the fourth comprises the relative success of the organization.

The aspects of technology utilized in the analysis were proposed by Dubin in 1959.[13] Woodward summarizes Dubin's discussion in her 1965 publication:

> Dubin (1959) said that technology is the most important single determinant of working behavior. He also defined his use of the word technology by subdividing it into two major phases: first, the tools, instruments, machines and technical formulas basic to the performance of the work; and secondly, the body of ideas which expresses the goals of the work, its functional importance, and the rationale of the methods employed.[14]

The relation theorized to obtain between technology and organization by Woodward may be represented schematically:

Primary Technology → adaptation of organizational forms required by primary technology → success.
Primary Technology → lack of adaptation of required organizational forms → lack of success.

The utilization of a specific type of primary technology may flow either from the desire to "modernize" operations (i.e., shift to mass production) or from the desire to produce high-quality, complex products possible only in small batch- or unit-production systems. Lack of success could result either from discrepancies between production goals and the primary technology or from discrepancies between primary technology and social organization.

The major organizational variables considered in the English study were: style of management, span of control, number of levels in authority structure, specialization of management, line-staff arrangements, composition of labor force, centralization of decision making in the firms, and individuals versus team decision making.

For analyzing production technology, Woodward invented a scale of technological complexity ranging from the simplest form of production known, "production of units to customers' requirements," to the most complex, "continuous-flow production of liquids, gases, and crystalline substances."

The scale of production systems presented by Woodward is said to represent the sequence of historical development of various types of production systems and simultaneously to represent stages of increasing control over the production process. Nine types of production systems are included in Woodward's scale of increasing technological complexity. In Woodward's words:

> It will be seen that the first nine systems of production given in Figure 11 form a scale; they are listed in order of chronological development, and technical complexity; the production of unit articles to customers' individual requirements being the oldest and simplest form of manufacture,

and the continuous-flow production of dimensional products, the most advanced and most complicated. Moving along the scale from Systems I to IX, it becomes increasingly possible to exercise control over manufacturing operations, the physical limitations of production becoming better known and understood. Targets can be set and reached more effectively in continuous-flow production plants than they can in the most up-to-date and efficient batch production firms, and the factors likely to limit performance can be allowed for. However well-developed production control procedures may be in batch production firms, there will be a degree of uncertainty in the prediction of results. Production proceeds by drives and a continuous attempt is made to push back physical limitations by setting ever higher targets. The difficulties of exercising effective control, particularly of prototype manufacture, are greatest in unit production. It is almost impossible to predict the results of development work either in terms of time or money.

In general, it is also true to say that prediction and control are easier in the manufacture of dimensional production than in the manufacture of integral products.[15]

Having briefly considered the nature of Woodward's study, it is appropriate to summarize some of her major findings.

THE FINDINGS OF THE SOUTH EAST ESSEX STUDY

The nature and importance of Woodward's findings may best be most cogently presented by examining three sets of findings: the relationship between operational success of the manufacturing firms and organizational characteristics; the relationships between technology and organizational characteristics; and the relationship between technology, organizational characteristics, and operational success.

Organizational Characteristics and Operational Success

The initial phases of the data analysis in the South East Essex Study, as reported by Woodward, sought to determine the organizational correlates of successful operation. After the data have been gathered and the characteristics of the organizations described, the research workers: ". . . tried to find out not only how the firms studied were organized and operated, but whether any particular form of organization was associated with management efficiency and commercial success."[16]

The results of the attempts to establish the organizational characteristics of successful firms were negative. The English researchers were unable to find organizational characteristics that were generally associated with operating success.[17]

Having failed to establish organizational correlates of success and an optimal form of organization, the investigators undertook an analysis of the technology of the firms.

Technology and Organization

After having developed the scale of increasing technological complexity, the investigation shifted to a consideration of the correlates of various types of production systems. Although the scale of technological complexity included a specification of nine types of production systems, these were, for purposes of analysis, combined into three major categories: unit and small-batch production systems, large-batch and mass-production systems, and continuous-flow process production systems. The analysis centered about a comparison of the organizational characteristics of the firms in each of these three major categories.

The analysis of the relationship between technology and organization yielded the specification of two patterns of association between technology and organization, together with a number of findings relating specific organizational characteristics and type of production system.

It was observed that in some cases organizational characteristics were directly related to the scale of technology. Unit and small-batch operations differed most from process operations, with the organizational characteristics of large-batch and mass-production firms falling between those of the extremes.

In other cases it was observed that the organization at the extremities of the scale (unit and process firms) resembled each other, while both differed organizationally from large-batch and mass-production firms.[18]

In addition to describing these two patterns of relationship between organization and technological complexity, a number of specific findings were presented to document the argument of a direct linkage between social organization and technology. Most of the analysis of the English study dealt with three types of organizational variables: general style of management, form and shape of organization, and composition of labor force.

Style of management. A distinction was made between organic and mechanistic management systems based upon degree of specification of tasks, responsibilities, and formalization of organization. Those organizations characterized by a high degree of formalization of management were called *mechanistic,* while those with less formalized management operations were labeled *organic* types.

Unit and process firms resembled one another in being most likely to have organic management systems, whereas mechanistic types predominated among large-batch and mass-production operations.

Shape and form of the organization. Several of the organizational characteristics examined by Woodward were related to the shape or form of the overall organizational structure. Included here were number of levels of management; span of control of first-line supervisors; span of control of top executives; internal divisions of organization along staff-line and related lines of cleavage; and relative proportion of supervisory to nonsupervisory personnel.

Linkages between technology and these organizational variables were observed. However, they were of different types. Some were as direct relationships; others were linked to the extremes of the technological scale.

The number of levels of management increased with increasing technological complexity, as did span of control of chief executive. The ratio of nonsupervisory personnel to supervisory personnel decreased as one moved up the scale of technology.

Span of control of first-line supervisors, on the other hand, was similar for process and unit operations and was greatest for the firms in the middle, large-batch, and mass-production categories.

Labor force. A number of the variables considered were either direct specifications of the nature of the labor force or related to labor policies and the allocation of resources within the firms.

All the relationships observed here (between technology and the ratio of direct to indirect labor; technology and advancement policies; technology and labor costs; technology and educational hiring policies; technology and ratio of production to maintenance workers) were direct, with unit and process firms differing most from one another, while large-batch and mass-production firms fell *between the extremities* with regard to the values of these variables.

The ratio of direct to indirect labor decreased as one moved from unit to process firms, as was true for percent of costs allocated to wages within the firms.

In unit-operation firms advancement policy was to promote almost exclusively from within; large-batch and mass-production firms were considerably more likely to look to the outside for filling vacancies; some process firms were inclined to hire from the outside rather than promote from within.

The merits of the study conducted by Woodward and associates and its relevance to the field of social organization are already apparent from the above review. But her findings are also important because they bring into question some notions widely held by organizational theorists.

For instance, when Woodward reported negative results in the initial search for organizational correlates of success, she included in this negative evaluation an analysis of the size of the labor force. The presumed importance of size, as measured by number of persons in the organization or other similar indexes, is well illustrated by reference to Caplow's evaluation of the importance of this variable: "Not only does the size of an organization affect all phases of its activity. . . . It is unrealistic, for example, to discuss manufacturing establishments without making a classificatory distinction between small workshops and giant factories."[19]

However, the English research reveals no relationship between size and organizational characteristics or operating success. Given the rather surprising nature of some of her findings and the obvious importance of the study, further research in this area is in order.

Woodward's analysis is the only systematic empirical analysis, case studies excluded, of technology and formal organization.* These findings are being received with considerable interest among organizational theorists,[20] but a replication is needed within the context and conditions of

---

* Two recent studies by Harvey and Rushing relate very closely to this kind of analysis. In Harvey's study the major difference is that the focus is on a variable which is assumed, probably with very good cause, to represent an important index of certain critical technological variables —change of product line. There is, however, no explicit concern with either a typology or with a multivariate analysis of the entire technological system. See Edward Harvey, "Technology and the Structure of Organizations," *American Sociological Review* 33 (April, 1968):247–259.

In Rushing's study there is a discussion of the relationship of technology (including an attempt to begin to break down Woodward's typology in a dimensional sort of way) to the observed correlations between material hardness and the division of labor. In this case the full data on technology are not presented although they were obviously gathered and will hopefully appear very shortly. See William A. Rushing, "Hardness of Material as Related to Division of Labor in Manufacturing Industries," *Administrative Science Quarterly* 13 (September, 1968): 229–245.

American economic institutions. Moreover, other factors than those considered by Woodward need to be investigated. The present study is a partial replication with extensions of the analysis presented by Woodward.

PROPOSED REPLICATION AND EXTENSION OF THE ESSEX STUDY

This replication accepts the conceptual scheme presented by Woodward and treats her findings as hypotheses. The replication differs, however, with respect to the characteristics of the firms included in the sample and with the socioeconomic setting of the firms: it also includes several variables not considered by Woodward. This study is therefore not an exact replication of Woodward's analysis. That portion which does correspond with her study provides us with a higher level of confidence in Woodward's conclusions, while the new variables introduced permit us to extend the Woodward findings in new directions.

Woodward's study has the general properties of a field survey of technology, industrial organization, and productive effectiveness in the Essex area. However, the study, so far as it goes beyond bare description toward the establishment of precise relationships, is essentially comparative. The critical question in every comparative study is the isolation of the structures compared. At present some of the best thought on this question is still to be found in Max Weber's essay on "Objectivity in Social Science and Social Policy."[21]

Weber has proposed the use of ideal types as a device for analyzing historical or survey material.

> An ideal type is formed by the one-sided accentuation of one or more points of view and by the synthesis of a great many diffuse, discrete, more or less present and occasionally absent *concrete individual* phenomena, which are arranged according to those one-sidedly emphasized viewpoints into a unified *analytical* construct.[22]

The function of such an ideal type was to make characteristic features of a phenomenon under investigation empirically clear. It is not a description of reality though it aims at making description unambiguously clear. It is not a hypothesis, though it aims to assist the formulation of hypotheses. It is not a model of what ought to exist, being ideal in the strictly logical sense of the term.

> It is a matter here of constructing relationships which our imagination accepts as plausibly motivated and hence as "objectively possible" and which appear as "adequate" from the nomological standpoint.[23]

In short, an ideal type consists of a provisional synthesis of our ideas about the nature of the phenomena under investigation and of the factors or variables appearing to be determinative of its character. Such an ideal type then facilitates the task of comparison by isolating configurations of factors presumed essential. Simultaneously, then, factors are isolated for precise description, and the analysis of possible relationships with other factors.

That Woodward's procedure was essentially ideal typical is shown by her isolation of three general types of production systems theorized to have differential organizational effects: unit- and small-batch production, large-batch and mass productions, and process production. These types were, in turn, associated with a number of factors (variables) deemed to be typical of technology and organization; size of labor force, technology, separation of ownership and management, promotion policy, type of management system, number of authority levels, span of control of chief executive and production supervisor, ratio of direct to indirect workers, and ratio of supervisory to nonsupervisory personnel.

In proposing a replication and extension of Woodward's study, the present researcher takes over her general typology and most of the factors and variables she employed, along with some additional values felt also to be relevant. They are as follows:

Variables in the Analysis

Three independent variables and four sets of dependent variables are utilized in the analysis. The dependent variables are grouped into the following categories: style of management, shape and form of organization, labor force, and ties to local community.

Independent variables. Type of production system was the independent variable in the Woodward studies. In addition to considering this factor, the analysis also considers size of labor force and relationship of ownership and management as potential determinants of organizational characteristics.

The findings reported regarding the lack of relationship between size of labor force and specific organizational characteristics are sufficiently surprising and important to warrant reconsideration in this context.

The relationship of ownership to management, separated or combined, is often cited as a factor affecting the characteristics and operations of industrial organizations.[24] In the case of the English study a consideration of the factor was not possible because of the lack of instances of combined ownership and management.[25]

Style of management. The distinction between organic and mechanistic management systems will serve as an index to management style.

Shape and form of the organization. Four variables related to the form of the organization are considered: number of levels in management hierarchy; span of control of chief executive; span of control of first-line supervisor; and ratio of nonsupervisory to supervisory personnel.

Labor force. Four variables related to the labor force are investigated: ratio of production to nonproduction workers; proportion of costs allocated to wages; promotion policy of firms; and ratio of nonmanagerial supervisors to managers.

Dependence on local markets. The relationship of organizations to other social units is a general concern within the field of sociology. It has been considered sufficiently important to warrant a consideration of the division of all studies into those that recognize and utilize the interdependence of social units in their analysis as opposed to those that treat the organization as a self-contained unit.[26] Woodward did not consider this in her analysis, but some attention may well be devoted to this persistent and difficult problem.

In order to maintain continuity with the English work, one variable was selected which is related both to the general question of community ties and to the Woodward analysis: an estimate of the importance of local markets for supplies and for sales.

Woodward's basic typology of technology is built around the idea of the control and predictability of production and the scheduling of production. Unit firms have the least controllable production, and it would seem as a consequence that they would be most likely to be dependent upon local markets for the supply of production materials, their production needs not being easily predicted. Process firms supply the needs of what we might call universal buyers, i.e., buyers that remain standard over space and time. Hence they are also usually in a position where they can exploit the total market for their supplies in a way usually not practicable for unit firms. In similar fashion the obverse of the above is argued in Chapter 6.

In addition to the three independent variables and the four types of dependent variables, one other organizational factor is carried through the analysis. This is the question of operating success, the consideration which led Woodward to her analysis of technology and to her major findings.

The Minneapolis Sample

The present analysis is based on data collected from 55 firms in the Minneapolis–St. Paul metropolitan area. These do not represent a probability sample of the firms in this area, and a census was out of the question, there being about 2,400 manufacturing firms in the metropolitan area.[27]

By way of contrast, the southeast Essex sample consisted of 100 firms, 91 percent of all firms in the area with a labor force of 100 or greater. The Essex firms covered a wide range of industrial sectors, but were concentrated in areas of recent industrial development, e.g., electronics and chemicals. They also tended to be newer firms, consistent with the late industrialization of this area.[28]

The major differences between the English and Minneapolis sample, aside from the question of sampling or census survey, are the range of industrial sectors represented and the proportion of firms with combined ownership and management. While no data are presented, Woodward does comment on the concentration of industries in the newer industrial sectors. By way of contrast it may be noted that the 55 firms in the Minneapolis sample are drawn from 18 of the major industrial sectors used in the Standard Industrial Classification of firms, the majority of sectors covering manufacturing firms.

In gathering data for the Minneapolis study[29] 70 firms were contacted. There were two refusals to provide information, and one interviewer was delayed sufficiently to force the selection of another firm. Of the 67 firms investigated, the interviewers were unable to obtain usable information on two of the firms; two other firms had such a mix of production technologies that they could not be included in the analysis. Eight of the remaining 63 firms had labor forces of less than 100 and were dropped from the analysis for the same reasons that Woodward dropped these smaller firms—the presence of only embryonic formal organizations.[30] This left 55 firms in the Minneapolis sample.

Hypotheses

The hypotheses guiding this study are the findings of the Woodward analysis.

In a replication the normal course of action is to take the findings of the previous study and to treat these as hypotheses in the replication. The relationships Woodward observed between technology and various organizational characteristics and the lack of relationships between organizational characteristics and size of the labor force thus become our hypotheses. We shall, independently of Woodward, add hypotheses concerning the relations between organizational characteristics and the separation of ownership and management.

It is also hypothesized that the relationship between the independent variables and the dependent variables will normally be manifested when evaluating all firms in the sample, but that these relationships may be strongest when analyzing only the more successful firms within the sample.

Plan of Analysis

Chapter 2 consists of a replication of Woodward's analysis of the relationship between operational success and organizational characteristics. Incidental to the major concern of Chapter 2 is a more detailed comparison of the organizational characteristics of the Essex and the Minneapolis firms.

Chapters 3, 4, 5, and 6 consider each of the sets of dependent variables being examined in this analysis. In these analytic chapters the hypotheses proposed between each of the independent variables and the dependent variables will be examined. The form of the analysis is to move from the most abstract characteristics of the organization to the most concrete, and to conclude with a consideration of the ties to the local community.

NOTES

1. Joan Woodward, *Industrial Organization: Theory and Practice* (London: Oxford University Press, 1965); idem, *Management and Technology,* Problems of Progress in Industry, No. 3 (London: Her Majesty's Stationery Office, Department of Scientific and Industrial Research, 1958).

2. An early and still widely cited classic statement of this position is found in Chester Barnard, *The Functions of the Executive* (Cambridge, Mass.: Harvard University Press, 1938). Although Barnard recognized the existence and general import of technologies in the context of formal organization, he viewed these either as creating limitations by restricting certain types of possible organizational arrangement (such as limiting the kind and quantity of communication) or as creating problems involving the coordination of these technologies in the context of the organization. His unquestioned emphasis was upon a conception of the organization as a set of cooperative relationships resting upon an adequate communication and decisional structure. For his evaluation of the role of technology in formal organizations, see, for example, pp. 90ff, 236ff.

3. Karl Marx, *Capital: A Critique of Political Economy* (1906; reprinted, New York: The Modern Library, n.d.), pp. 458–459.

4. Ibid., p. 461.

5. Ibid., p. 463.

6. Ely Chinoy, *Automobile Workers and the American Dream* (New York: Doubleday & Company, 1955); Charles R. Walker and Robert H. Guest, *The Man on the Assembly Line* (Cambridge, Mass.: Harvard University Press, 1952). Walker's continuing concern with the relationship between technology and formal organization provides one of the most prominent exceptions to the dominant trend in the field of formal organization.

7. Alvin W. Gouldner, "Metaphysical Pathos and the Theory of Bureaucracy," *American Political Science Review* 49 (1955): 501.

8. See Martin Meissner, "Behavioral Adaptations to Industrial Technology" (Ph.D. dissertation, University of Oregon, 1964); and James D. Thompson, *Organizations in Action* (New York: McGraw-Hill Book Company, 1967).

9. Among American students of organization, who have generally tended to play down the significance of technology or to ignore it altogether, Robert Dubin is a notable exception. In *The World of Work: Industrial Society and Human Relations* (Englewood Cliffs, N.J.: Prentice-Hall, 1958), pp. 61–76, Dubin emphasizes the importance of technology, viewing it as one of the four basic behavior systems of social organizations. He also again emphasizes the importance of technology for an understanding of human interaction in *Leadership and Productivity: Some Facts of Industrial Life* (San Francisco: Chandler Publishing Company, 1965), chap. 1.

10. Wilbur E. Moore, *The Impact of Industry* (Englewood Cliffs, N.J.: Prentice-Hall, 1965), p. 4.

11. Joan Woodward, *Management and Technology*. For a consideration of the relationship between technology and formal organization in nonindustrial societies, see Stanley H. Udy, Jr., *Organization of Work: A Comparative Analysis of Production Among Nonindustrial Peoples* (New York: Taplinger Publishing Company, 1959).

12. Woodward, *Industrial Organization.*

13. Robert Dubin, *Working Union-Management Relations; The Sociology of Industrial Relations* (Englewood Cliffs, N.J.: Prentice-Hall, 1959).

14. Woodward, *Industrial Organization,* p. 36.

15. Ibid., p. 40.

16. Ibid., p. 14.

17. Ibid., pp. 33–34.

18. Ibid., p. 51.

19. Theodore Caplow, *Principles of Organization* (New York: Harcourt, Brace & World, 1964), p. 26.

20. See, for example, Robert Dubin, "Supervision and Productivity: Empirical Findings and Theoretical Considerations" in Robert Dubin et al., *Leadership and Productivity: Some Facts of Industrial Life* (San Francisco: Chandler Publishing Company, 1965); James D. Thompson, *Organizations in Action* (New York: McGraw-Hill Book Company, 1967); Charles Perrow, "A Framework for the Comparative Analysis of Organizations," *American Sociological Review* 32 (April, 1967):194–208; idem, *Review of Industrial Organization: Theory and Practice* by Joan Woodward, *American Sociological Review* 32 (April, 1967): 313–315.

21. Max Weber, *The Methodology of the Social Sciences,* trans. Edward A. Shils and Henry A. Finch (New York: The Free Press, 1949), pp. 50ff.

22. Ibid., p. 90.

23. Ibid., p. 92.

24. See, for example, "The Executive and the Owner-Entrepreneur," in *Reader in Bureaucracy,* ed. Robert K. Merton et al. (New York: The Free Press, 1952), pp. 158–164.

25. Woodward, *Industrial Organization*, p. 8.

26. See, for example, Alvin W. Gouldner, "Organizational Analysis," in *Sociology Today* ed. Robert K. Merton, Leonard Broom, and Leonard S. Cottrell, Jr. (New York: The Free Press, 1954); James D. Thompson, *Organizations in Action* (New York: McGraw-Hill Book Company, 1967), esp. pp. 3–10; Stanley H. Udy, Jr., "The Comparative Analysis of Organizations," in *Handbook of Organizations* ed. James G. March (Chicago: Rand McNally & Company, 1965), pp. 678–709; William R. Dill, "Business Organizations," in ibid., pp. 1071–1114; and Chadwick J. Haberstroh, "Organization Design and Systems Analysis," in ibid., pp. 1071–1212.

27. Information obtained from the Director of Research, Department of Employment Security, State of Minnesota. This estimate was based on data collected in May 1966.

28. Woodward, *Industrial Organization*, pp. 6–10.

29. A short note on general methodological considerations will be found in Appendix 1.

30. Woodward, *Industrial Organization*, p. 9.

2

THE ORGANIZATIONAL CHARACTERISTICS OF ENGLISH AND MIDWESTERN AMERICAN INDUSTRIES

Following the procedure of Woodward and her associates, the replication and extension of the study of industrial operations in South East Essex begins with the search for possible organizational correlates of successful industrial operations.

In organizational analysis the concept of "success" plays a role roughly comparable to "happiness" in the older analyses of marriage and the family. Success is conventionally visualized as the goal, aim, or object of industrial organizations in somewhat the same manner as happiness is commonly taken as the aim of marriage. One difference between organizational analysts and the earlier students of marriage and the family is that those who pursued the elusive goal of happiness always knew that there might be different routes to the attainment of this state, whereas organizational analysts have been prone to search for one route to organizational success.

One need not be disturbed if in the analysis of economic organizations there are a variety of routes to success, depending on circumstances. However, it is important here, as in the analysis of the family, to know what meaning is assigned to the concept since it provides the initial orientation of the analysis.

In the English study "success" was conceived in judgmental and financial terms. The final classification utilized by Woodward divided the firms into three categories: above-average success, average success, and below-average success.[1] The criteria used for making these evaluations were evaluations by others in the industry as well as assessments of fiscal operations. This approach appears to be reasonable in an economy which is "tight,"[2] but less so in an economy of affluence.

In an affluence economy there are few failures and success is more relevant to the extent to which the organization is achieving maximum efficiency or is satisfied with mere "safe" level of accomplishment.[3]

If a maximizing criteria of success is utilized, a relational evaluation is appropriate. If the organizations are striving for mere satisfactory levels of performance, relational evaluations may be of little use.

The economic situation of Minneapolis industries is quite favorable. A rather thoroughgoing search for bona fide examples of manufacturing failures[4] covering the period 1966–67, yielded one division of one corporation employing more than 100 persons which could be so classified. Whereas the situation in England is polarized between the haves and have-nots, the situation in Minneapolis is loosely divided between the more affluent and the less affluent.

The most practical approach to industrial success in the Minneapolis area is in terms of a division between organizations with virtually windfall profits and those with normal profits. This is quite literally a case of distinguishing between the fat and the well-fed.

Because of the extraordinarily benign economic milieu of the Twin City Metropolitan area, those industries which were obviously successful in every respect, which in recent history reaped high profits, and which enaged in major capital expansion programs were labeled "very successful."[5] Those industries which were merely getting by, enjoying normal profits and expanding at a traditional pace, were labeled "less successful."

In the sample of 55 Minneapolis firms the "least" successful firm had recently experienced a sudden change of management accompanied by a loss during this year. The loss, incidentally, was quickly made up the following year. One other firm is known locally for its sluggish operation, but was recently purchased by an outside corporation which is pouring money into it. All prospects look rosy for the next several years of its operation.

The procedure in this chapter, then, is to compare the organizational characteristics of very successful Minneapolis firms with those of the less successful firms. This in turn will permit comparison with Woodward's general finding regarding the lack of correlation between organizational characteristics and operational success in her study at Essex. Incidental to this, a comparison of the Minneapolis data with those of the English sample is made to ascertain the general comparability of the two samples.

The organizational variables are grouped in the same manner as previously—independent variables, style of management, form and shape of the organization, labor force, and ties to the community.

INDEPENDENT VARIABLES

As noted earlier, Woodward attempted to construct a scale of increasing technological complexity for the analysis of the southeast Essex data. The scale consisted of the specification of nine types of production systems which were then grouped into three major types for the purpose of analysis. The major divisions of production systems and their associated specific types are:

Unit and Small-Batch Production
   1. Production of units to customers' requirements
   2. Production of prototypes
   3. Fabrication of large equipment in stages
   4. Production of small batches to customers' orders
Large-Batch and Mass Production
   5. Production of large batches
   6. Production of large batches on assembly line
   7. Mass production

Process Production
  8. Intermittent production of chemicals in multipurpose plant
  9. Continuous-flow production of liquids, gases, and crystalline substances

A comment or two is perhaps in order on this so-called scale of increasing technological complexity. Strictly speaking, a full true scale comprises some single measurable property whose units are operationalized in such matter that it is legitimate to add, subtract, multiply, and divide them. Or one may legitimately isolate a partial or ordinal scale if one can at least specify some operation by which various points along it may legitimately be ordered as more or less in a single direction.

It requires little reflection to ascertain that Woodward's nine-point scale of technical complexity fits the requirements of neither a full nor a partial (ordinal) scale. It is quite possible that, for example, the production of small batches to customers' orders (point 4) could be less technically complex than the production of units to customers' requirements (point 1). One could isolate numerous other possible anomalies in Woodward's nine-point scale.

The only fair estimate of Woodward's practice is that this phase of her study was a product of the popularity of the general sociological pastime of scale construction. However this may be, it is only fair to go along as far as one can with Woodward's presentation of her materials in the form of a scale—although, in fact, her analysis is basically typological.[6]

A detailed breakdown of the distribution of American and English firms within each of the nine production categories is presented in Appendix 3, Table 29. The analysis here will focus on considerations of the three major divisions or types of production system—unit and small-batch, large-batch and mass production, and process production.[7]

Woodward observed no association between success of the firms operation and types of production system, 22 percent (5/24) of the unit operations, 16 percent (5/31) of the large batch, and 24 percent (6/25) of the process firms were rated as above average in success. Analogous findings were observed for the Minneapolis firms. Using a different system for rating success[8] 53 percent (10/19) of the unit firms, and 50 percent (15/30) of the large-batch operations were rated as very successful. All of the process firms in the Minneapolis sample were rated as very successful, but because there were only six of these they cannot serve to confirm or negate any of the English findings except in an anecdotal fashion (Table 1). No relationships were observed between the type of production system and the success of the firms' operations.

The major differences observed between the distribution of technologies in the English and Minneapolis samples were the relatively greater proportion of large-batch and mass-production firms found in the Twin Cities area and the smaller proportion of process firms found in the Minneapolis sample, 32 percent (25/80) of the English firms had process production systems compared with only 11 percent (6/55) of the American firms, and 39 percent (31/80) of the English firms were large-batch and mass-production operations compared with over half of the Minneapolis firms, 55 percent (30/55). This difference is a function of the industrial histories and potential of the two areas with respect to markets and available resources (Table 1).

It should be noted that in both studies the assessment

TABLE 1

PRODUCTION TECHNOLOGY AND LEVEL OF BUSINESS SUCCESS IN MINNEAPOLIS AND ESSEX FIRMS

LEVEL OF SUCCESS	TECHNOLOGY[a]					
	Unit and Small-Batch		Large-Batch and Mass		Process	
	No.	%	No.	%	No.	%
Minneapolis Firms						
Very successful	10	53	15	50	6	100
Less successful	9	47	15	50	—	—
Total	19	100	30	100	6	100
Essex Firms[b]						
Above-average success	5	21	5	16	6	24
Average success	14	58	20	65	15	60
Below-average success	5	21	6	19	4	16
Total	24	100	31	100	25	100

[a] χ^2 (for Minneapolis firms) = 5.26 (df = 2), $p < .10$.
[b] Joan Woodward, *Industrial Organization* (London: Oxford University Press, 1965), p. 39.

of the relative success of the firms was made prior to the data analysis itself.

In examining the relationship between size of labor force and operating success, it should be noted that Woodward did not provide an explicit statement on this matter. The implication of her analysis is that no association between size of labor force and operating success was observed in the Essex study.

In the case of the Minneapolis firms, there was observable a possible relationship between success and size, the breaking point occurring between rather large firms as compared with rather small ones: 75 percent (15/20) of the firms with over 1,000 employees were very successful compared with 46 percent (16/35) of those with fewer than 1,000 (Table 2). The implications of this for the analysis of the relationship between the independent variables and organizational characteristics are not clear at this point.

TABLE 2

SIZE OF LABOR FORCE AND LEVEL OF BUSINESS SUCCESS IN MINNEAPOLIS FIRMS

LEVEL OF SUCCESS	SIZE OF LABOR FORCE[a]					
	100–250[b]		251–1,000		More than 1,000	
	No.	%	No.	%	No.	%
Very successful	8	44	8	47	15	75
Less successful	10	56	9	53	5	25
Total	18	100	17	100	20	100

[a] $\chi^2 = 4.480$ (df = 1), $p < .05$ (when firms with 1,000 or fewer employees are compared to those with more than 1,000 employees).
[b] The size categories are those utilized by Woodward and are retained in order to maintain continuity between the two analyses.

Further investigation of the relationship between size and operating success reveals that the original finding was replicated when size and technology were considered simultaneously: 80 percent (4/5) of the large compared with 43 percent (6/14) of the smaller unit and small-batch operations are very successful and 67 percent (8/12) of the large compared with 39 percent (7/18) of the smaller large-batch and mass-production firms were rated very successful (Appendix 3, Table 30).

Regardless of the final interpretation assigned to this relationship these findings do represent a potentially significant difference between the Minneapolis and English analyses.

With respect to the overall distribution of size within the Minneapolis and English samples, it should be noted that the American sample contained a considerably greater proportion of firms with labor forces greater than 1,000 than did the English sample—56 percent (20/55) compared with 15 percent (12/80).[9]

The final independent variable being considered is the relationship between ownership and management. No comparison between the Minneapolis and Essex sample was possible here due to the absence of instances of combined ownership and management in the English sample.

Here, as was the case with respect to size of the labor force, there appeared to be a relationship between operating success and ownership and management. Less than half of the firms with combined ownership and management were very successful—38 percent (6/16), compared with about 2/3 of those with separated ownership and management, which represented 64 percent (25/39) (Table 3).

The relationship between ownership, management, and success appeared to be partially a product of the fact that most of the firms with combined ownership and management were relatively small operations, none having a labor force in excess of 1,000. Among the smaller firms, 38 percent

(6/16) of those with combined ownership and management were very successful compared with 53 percent (10/19) of those with separated ownership and management (Appendix 3, Table 31).

TABLE 3

SEPARATION OF OWNERSHIP AND MANAGEMENT AND LEVEL OF BUSINESS SUCCESS IN MINNEAPOLIS FIRMS

LEVEL OF SUCCESS	OWNERSHIP AND MANAGEMENT[a]			
	Combined		Separated	
	No.	%	No.	%
Very successful	6	38	25	64
Less successful	10	62	14	36
Total	16	100	39	100

[a] $\chi^2 = 3.264$ (df = 1), $p < .10$.

Among the independent variables both size of the labor force and the separation of ownership and management appear to be linked to operating success. Given the growth pattern of successful firms, the general tendency toward an increase in scale of organizations in contemporary society, and the ability of these firms to use their greater capital resources to ride out lean periods, there is no reason to be particularly surprised by this result. A number of the smaller firms are very successful, but given the propensity for successful firms to grow in an expanding economy and the movement toward continual merger, this kind of association should be expected.

What is of greater interest in this analysis are the links between specific organizational characteristics and success, and eventually between these organizational characteristics, viewed as dependent variables, and the independent variables. With this in mind we may now turn to a consideration of the relationship between operating success and the dependent variables, beginning with a consideration of style of management.

STYLE OF MANAGEMENT

Dividing the firms into those with organic management systems and those with mechanistic management systems it was found that 28 could be classified as organic, 18 as mechanistic, and 9 as mixed. This overall distribution appears quite similar to that found by Woodward in view of her comment that about twice as many of her firms had organic management systems as had mechanistic systems.[10]

No relationship was observed between type of management system and operating success, 54 percent (15/28) of the firms with organic systems were very successful compared with 67 percent (12/18) of those with mechanistic systems (Appendix 3, Table 32).

This finding is consistent with that reported by Woodward with respect to the relationship between shape and form of organization and operating success.

SHAPE AND FORM OF THE ORGANIZATION

Four organizational characteristics were considered with respect to the form of organization: number of levels in the management hierarchy; span of control of chief executive; span of control of first-line supervisor; and number of non-supervisory workers for each supervisor.

Success and hierarchy. No association between success and number of levels of the management hierarchy was observed among the Minneapolis firms.[11] The median for the very successful Minneapolis firms was five management levels and the range was 3–7; the median for the less successful firms was 4.5, and the range was 3–8 (Appendix 3, Table 33).

The English firms studied by Woodward had a greater range of management levels than do the Minneapolis firms; 2–10 versus 3–8. However, the medians and clustering were similar, being 4 for the Essex firms and 5 for the Minneapolis firms.[12]

Span of control of chief executive. Span of control of chief executive[13] was very similar for both the very successful and the less successful Minneapolis firms, as well as for the Essex[14] and the Minneapolis firms (Appendix 3, Table 34). No association between this variable and success was found.

Span of control of first-line supervisor. Similar lack of association was observed with respect to success and span of control of first-line supervisor.[15] The median number of persons under the control of the first-line supervisor for the very successful and less successful Minneapolis firms was 20. About half of the firms had spans of control between 11 and 20; about two-thirds of the firms had spans of control under 30 (Appendix 3, Table 35).

The Essex and the Minneapolis firms were quite different in the spans of control of their respective first-line supervisors. The median for the English firms was considerably higher, about 28. About half of the English firms had spans of 21–50. The range for the English firms was also considerably greater than their Minneapolis counterparts, with a greater number having large spans of control.[16]

Number of nonsupervisory personnel per supervisor. The final variable to be considered here is the number of nonsupervisory persons for each supervisor.[17] A hint of association between success and this organizational characteristic was indicated when the median for the very successful Minneapolis firms showed about 9, while that for the less successful firms was about 13. The distributions for very successful and less successful firms were sufficiently similar, however, to warrant the conclusion that they are essentially the same—61 percent (17/28) of the very successful firms and

58 percent (14/24) of the less successful firms had ratios between 5 and 14 (Appendix 3, Table 36).

The relative number of nonsupervisory personnel for the English firms was somewhat greater, a finding predictable from the previous observation that the span of control of first-line supervisors tended to be considerably greater for Essex firms than for the Minneapolis firms.[18]

The Minneapolis data on the four organizational characteristics supported the general finding reported by Woodward in regard to the lack of correlation between specific organizational variables and operating success. The four variables related to labor force and the items related to community ties remain to be examined.

LABOR FORCE

Of the four organizational variables regarding the labor force, only one—promotion policy—revealed association with operational success.

Ratios of production worker. The ratio of production to nonproduction workers was not associated with operational success. The median for the very successful firms was 2.0, compared with 3.0 for the less successful firms. Similar ranges of values were observed for both sets of firms, the only difference being that all firms with ratios of less than one were very successful operations (Appendix 3, Table 37).

The distributions of values and the medians were very similar for the Essex and the Minneapolis samples indicating comparability with respect to this variable.[19]

Ratio of nonmanagerial supervisors to managers. The relative numbers of managers to nonmanagerial supervisors did not appear to be related to success. The median number of nonmanagerial supervisors for each manager was two for both the very successful and the less successful Minneapolis firms (Appendix 3, Table 38). No information on this variable was presented in the English study.

Wage-cost allocations. The percent of costs allocated to wages did not appear to be linked to operating success for the Minneapolis firms. The median for the very successful and the less successful firms falls between 26 and 50 percent; the distribution of values for the two sets of firms is quite similar (Appendix 3, Table 39).

Labor costs of the Essex firms tend to be somewhat lower than for Minneapolis firms.[20] This finding is consistent with the lower ratio of supervisory personnel in the English firms, the difference in general wage conditions obtaining between the two nations, and the greater proportion of process firms in the Essex sample.

Promotion policies. The promotion policies of the Minneapolis firms varied in terms of their inclination to promote from within or to hire from the outside to fill vacancies within the administrative structure. No Minneapolis firm studied reported a policy of hiring from the outside, although 34 percent (19/55) report a mixed policy while the remaining 66 percent (36) attempted to fill vacancies from within the organization. A somewhat greater proportion of those firms that had a policy of promoting from within were very successful—61 percent (22/36)—than did those with a mixed policy, 47 percent (9/19) (Appendix 3, Table 40). This difference is not statistically significant but is sufficiently great at first glance to warrant noting.

The examination of the relationship between the variables relating to the labor force and operating success supported Woodward's negative findings, as was the case with respect to style of management and the variables relating to shape and form of organization and operating success.

TIES TO THE COMMUNITY

The two variables chosen to indicate ties to the community are the extent of reliance on local markets either for production supplies or for sales.

Neither of these variables appeared to be related to operating success in any way. Fifty-seven percent (16/28) of the firms that relied significantly on the local community for production materials were very successful compared with 56 percent (15/27) of those that did not (Appendix 3, Table 41). Fifty-nine percent (13/22) of the firms that relied on local markets for a significant portion of their sales were very successful, compared with 55 percent (18/33) of those that sold predominately outside of the local marketing area (Appendix 3, Table 42).

SUMMARY

It should first be noted that Woodward's finding of a lack of relationship between specific organizational characteristics and operating success is confirmed in the Minneapolis replication. The major exceptions are the greater probability of success observed in the very large metropolitan firms, with labor forces in excess of one thousand and with ownership and management separated.

The relationship noted between success and separation of ownership and management proved, upon further examination, partially to result from a correlation between size and separation of ownership and management.

The only deviation from Woodward's findings was a weak relationship between promotion policy and success. A somewhat greater proportion of those firms with policies of promoting from within were very successful than was true for firms with a mixed advancement policy, 61 percent compared to 47 percent.

In the comparison of the organizational characteristics of the Essex and the Minneapolis firms some specific differences were observed, but there is little reason to assume that these firms are not basically similar. While some median values and ranges of values differed, the basic similarity suggests that the two samples are drawn essentially from the same types of industrial complex.

Having established tentative confirmation of Woodward's first general finding, it is time to turn to the analysis of the relationship between the independent and the dependent variables. This phase of the analysis will begin with a consideration of the general style of management, the most abstract of Woodward's organizational variables.

NOTES

1. Joan Woodward, *Industrial Organization* (London: Oxford University Press, 1965), pp. 14–16.

2. Operating under conditions of scarcity.

3. The distinction between maximizing and satisfying criteria of organizational evaluation was introduced in Herbert A. Simon, *Models of Man, Social and Rational* (New York: John Wiley & Sons, 1957). For a discussion of these criteria of evaluation in the context of general organizational theory, see James D. Thompson, *Organizations in Action* (New York: McGraw-Hill Book Company, 1967).

4. Industries raided and liquidated for immediate cash gains or those deliberately sent into receivership following the withdrawal of assets are not included as examples of bona fide industrial failures.

5. A specification of the criteria utilized in evaluating the success of the firms is presented in Appendix 7.

6. See, for example, Morris R. Cohen and Ernest Nagel, "Measurements," in *The Structure of Scientific Thought*, ed. Edward H. Madden (Boston: Houghton Mifflin Company, 1960), pp. 530ff.

7. This was in fact the procedure followed by Woodward in her analysis.

8. As described on pp. 17–19.

9. Woodward, *Industrial Organization*, p. 8.

10. Ibid., p. 24.

11. The number of levels in the management hierarchy has received considerable attention in the recent literature on organizations and the importance and evaluation of this organizational characteristics is considered in Chapter 4.

12. Woodward, *Industrial Organization*, p. 25.

13. Span of control is one of the most prominent variables in classical management theory. The position of this variable in the earlier organizational analysis and current interpretation of the importance and place of this variable in organizational analysis is considered in Chapter 4.

14. Woodward, *Industrial Organization*, p. 26.

15. A discussion of the position of this variable in organizational analysis, as is the case for span of control of chief executive, will be found in Chapter 4.

16. Woodward, *Industrial Organization*, p. 26.

17. Discussion of the variable, as is the case for the others relating to the form of the organization, is delayed until Chapter 4.

18. Woodward, *Industrial Organization*, p. 27.

19. Ibid., p. 29.

20. Ibid., p. 54.

3

TYPES OF MANAGEMENT SYSTEMS

In her initial study of the industrial complex of Essex, Woodward proposed to test the efficacy of classical management theory. The proposal, which was replicated in Chapter 1 on Minneapolis data, ended in disaster. A few words are in order about classical organization theory and the role it plays in Woodward's follow-up study reported in 1965.

WOODWARD'S USE OF CLASSICAL MANAGEMENT THEORY

In the reflections of the classical students, management is conceptualized as basically a line-staff structure[1] which can be broken down into such subproperties as: number of hierarchical levels, span of control of chief executive, span of control of first-line supervisors, etc. If the organization is of a commercial-industrial form, the ultimate test of the organization will be found in its capacity to survive and make profits. As a matter of fact, in the competition for economic survival, it was assumed that those organizations best able to adapt and trim themselves down to essentials will approximate the most efficient form.

This seems to have been the rationale for the original study: If one were simply to isolate the variables presupposed by classical theory and review the patterns of industrial success in terms of them, a maximum efficient model should emerge. However, the enterprise came to grief. In her initial report Woodward recounted this disaster, indicating that she had in fact reviewed numerous variables but was presenting only a few sample tables on the findings of some of the variables to illustrate the negative character of the findings in general.

The general effect of this unexpected turn of events was to force Woodward to place an emphasis on technology that had been remote from her intentions. But it also presented her with the problem of how to conceive the classical picture of organization, for she was by no means persuaded that it had to be scrapped. Woodward's response to this problem was to reconceptualize the classical model of management as only one type.

MECHANISTIC AND ORGANIC SYSTEMS

In her 1965 report Woodward isolates two major types of management systems: mechanistic and organic.[2]

The distinction between mechanistic and organic systems of management is of considerable sociological interest, since it is intimately related to concepts crucial to the development of the discipline. The description of the two types of systems is rather closely identified with Tönnies distinction between *Gemeinschaft* and *Gesellschaft*[3] and with Durkheim's distinction between mechanical and organic forms of solidarity.[4]

> "Mechanistic" systems are characterized by rigid breakdown into functional specialism, precise definition of duties, responsibilities and power, and a well developed command hierarchy through which information filters up and decisions and instructions flow down. "Organic" systems are more adaptable; jobs lose much of their formal definition, and communications up and down the hierarchy are more in the nature of consultation than of the passing up of information and the receiving of orders.[5]

The typology of management systems utilized by Woodward[6] is important for yet another reason central to our own analysis. As originally presented by Tönnies and maintained by those who followed in this tradition, the distinction between mechanical and organic systems was viewed as describing an evolutionary movement from organic systems to mechanistic systems. Thus the original statement of the general concepts carried with it the same historical focus as is implied in Woodward's "scale" of technological complexity. In addition, these concepts are closely related to a contemporary fear of the "dehumanizing" potential of technology, a fear which to a large extent centers on the prediction of a general dominance of mechanistic systems.

Given the importance of this distinction to Woodward's analysis, its close affinity to major historical concepts of sociology, and its possible relevance to widespread contemporary fears of dehumanization, it deserves special review here.

FACTORS DETERMINING MANAGEMENT TYPE

The number of firms with organic systems was considerably greater than those with mechanistic systems in both the Essex and the Minneapolis samples: 61 percent (28/46) in the Minneapolis sample[7] and about two-thirds of the Essex firms.[8]

Treating type of management system as a dependent

variable in the analysis of organizations, we may investigate the relationship between the presence or absence of one or the other type and the three variables suggested as possible determinants of organizational characteristics: relationship of ownership to management, size of labor force, and type of production technology.

Ownership and Management Type

The separation of management and ownership was historically an important factor in the rationalization of organizational operations. In the course of industrial development, management grew increasingly conscious of the problems of structure and the need to organize such structure in a manner effective for the attainment of management goals. The entrepreneur of early industrial history driven by whim and "intuition" contrasts sharply with the conservative professional manager more frequently encountered today—a manager guided by a rational evaluation of the needs of the organization.[9]

The imagery of the entrepreneur and the professional manager current in the literature and among the public at large suggests the hypothesis: *Mechanical management systems are associated with a separation of ownership and management, whereas organic management systems are associated with a combined ownership and management.*

From Table 4 a tendency was observed for firms with combined ownership and management to have organic management systems. However, there was no apparent tendency for firms with separate ownership and management to have mechanical systems.

Management Type and Labor Force

The second possible determinant of type of management system is size of labor force. It could be argued that sheer numbers necessitate a formalization of organizational relationships.[10] It is conceivable that organic systems can be operative only in small-scale organizational settings.[11] The following hypothesis is suggested: *The occurrence of mechanical management systems is a direct function of increasing size of the organization as measured by the number of persons in the organization, the converse being the case for organic systems.*

TABLE 4

SEPARATION OF OWNERSHIP AND MANAGEMENT AND TYPE OF MANAGEMENT SYSTEM IN MINNEAPOLIS FIRMS

MANAGEMENT SYSTEM	OWNERSHIP AND MANAGEMENT[a]			
	Combined		Separated	
	No.	%	No.	%
Organic	11	73	17	55
Mechanical	4	27	14	45
Total	15	100	31	100

[a] $\chi^2 = 1.45$ (df = 1), $p > .20$.

An examination of Table 5 reveals the presence of no statistically significant relationship. At most, the data are suggestive of a possible break in the association between size of the labor force and type of management system for the largest organizations, 71 percent (20/28) of the firms below 1,000 had organic management systems while only 44 percent (8/18) of those with more than 1,000 employees had organic systems.

TABLE 5

SIZE OF LABOR FORCE AND TYPE OF MANAGEMENT SYSTEM IN MINNEAPOLIS FIRMS

MANAGEMENT SYSTEM	SIZE OF LABOR FORCE[a]					
	100–250		251–1,000		More than 1.000	
	No.	%	No.	%	No.	%
Organic	10	71	10	71	8	44
Mechanical	4	29	4	29	10	56
Total	14	100	14	100	18	100

[a] $\chi^2 = 3.358$ (df = 2), p > .15.

The importance of the difference observed between firms with more than 1,000 employees and those with less than this number—the same break observed in the analysis of size and success—will be considered after we have made an analysis of the relationship between type of production system and type of management system.

Management Type and Production Technology

Woodward reported an association between production technology and type of management system.

There was a tendency for organic management systems to predominate in the production categories at the extremes of the technical scale, while mechanistic systems predominated in the middle ranges. Clear-cut definition of duties and responsibilities was characteristic of firms in the middle ranges, while flexible organization with a high degree of delegation both of authority and of the responsibility for decision-making, and with permissive and participating management, was characteristic of firms at the extremes.[12]

The findings of the English study suggest, then, this hypothesis: *Organic management systems predominate among unit and process production systems, whereas mechanistic management systems are associated with large-batch and mass-production systems.*

The data on the relationship between type of production system and type of management system are presented in Table 6. The data are supportive of the hypothesis. Eighty-eight percent (14/16) unit and small-batch operations and 75 percent (3/4) of the process firms had organic management systems, while only a minority of the large-batch and mass-production operations—42 percent (11/26)—had organic management systems. The χ^2 for this table is high, 9.88 at two degrees of freedom, $p < .01$.

It was noted previously that there appeared to be a possible association between organic management systems and combined ownership and management, and between very large organizations and mechanistic systems. It is possible, even with such a small group of firms, to begin to investigate these relationships by looking simultaneously at the relationship between type of management system and two of the proposed independent variables.

TABLE 6

PRODUCTION TECHNOLOGY AND TYPE OF MANAGEMENT SYSTEM IN MINNEAPOLIS FIRMS

MANAGEMENT SYSTEM	TECHNOLOGY[a]					
	Unit and Small-Batch		Large-Batch and Mass		Process	
	No.	%	No.	%	No.	%
Organic	14	88	11	42	3	75
Mechanical	2	12	15	58	1	25
Total	16	100	26	100	4	100

[a] $\chi^2 = 9.88$ (df $= 2$), $p < .01$.

If Woodward's interpretation of the importance of the relationship between type of production system and organizational characteristics is correct, then we should find that when firms with similar types of production systems are compared the relationship between type of production system and type of management system will be maintained regardless of variation with respect to the relationship of ownership and management, or size of labor force.

If, on the other hand, production technology is not the critical variable in this analysis, then we should expect to find firms which share similar production technologies but which differ with respect to the relationship between ownership and management, and size of labor force differing with respect to type of management system within the firms.

We will first consider the relative importance of type

of production system and relationship of ownership to management as determinants of the type of management system. In this case the data clearly support the hypothesis linking production technology and type of management system, and thus negates the hypothesis linking the separation of ownership and management to type of management system.

Among unit and small-batch operations the proportion of firms having organic management system was identical for those having combined ownership and management and those having separated ownership and management—7/8 in each case.

Among large-batch and mass-production firms the proportion having mechanistic system was very nearly the same for those firms with combined ownership and management—50 percent (3/6)—as it was for those with separated ownership and management, where the proportion was 60 percent (12/20).

These data on the Minneapolis firms support Woodward's original finding with respect to the relationship between type of production system and type of management system. The relative importance of type of production system and size of labor force must also be considered as possible determinants of the type of management system. Data bearing on this relationship are presented in Table 7. Since the break with respect to the importance of size seems to occur between firms with more than 1,000 employees and those with less, this division will be used in the presentation of data here.[13]

Proportions of unit and small-batch operations of different sizes having organic management systems were almost identical: 92 percent (11/12) of the smaller firms and 75

TABLE 7

PRODUCTION TECHNOLOGY, SIZE OF LABOR FORCE, AND TYPE OF MANAGEMENT SYSTEM IN MINNEAPOLIS FIRMS

	TECHNOLOGY[a]							
	UNIT AND SMALL-BATCH				LARGE-BATCH AND MASS			
	Size of Company Labor Force				Size of Company Labor Force			
	1,000 or less		More than 1,000		1,000 or less		More than 1,000	
MANAGEMENT SYSTEM	No.	%	No.	%	No.	%	No.	%
Organic	11	92	3	75	7	50	4	33
Mechanical	1	8	1	25	7	50	8	67
Total	12	100	4	100	14	100	12	100

[a] Process-production firms are omitted from this analysis because the type of management system characterizing these firms was known for only four of the six in the sample, four being far too few for this type of analysis.

percent (3/4) of the larger firms having organic systems. The proportion of large-batch and mass-production systems having mechanistic system varied only slightly with size: 50 percent (7/14) for the smaller firms and 67 percent (8/12) for the larger firms.

The relationship between type of production technology and type of management system is most clear when only the very successful firms are compared with one another: 90 percent (9/10) of the very successful unit and small-batch operations had organic systems; 77 percent (10/13) of the very successful large-batch and mass-production firms had mechanistic systems. Moreover, when only the very successful firms are considered, the relationship between size of labor force and type of management system all but vanished: all (6/6) of the smaller and 75 percent (3/4) of the successful unit and small-batch firms had organic systems. Among the very successful large-batch and mass-production firms 80 percent (4/5) of the smaller firms and 75 percent (6/8) of the larger firms had mechanistic systems.

The relationship between type of management system and the independent variables, separation of ownership and management, size of the labor force, and type of production technology, clearly indicates that: (1) production technology of the firm was strongly related to the type of management system; but (2) size of labor force and relationship of ownership to management were not. Moreover, the relationship between production technology and type of management system was strongest when only the very successful firms were examined—a finding which further supports Woodward's analysis of the impact of technology on industrial organization.[14]

SUMMARY

An important aspect of Woodward's study replicated on Minneapolis data is the modification of the classical conception of management. The failure of the initial attempt to correlate variables significant for the classical (formalized line-staff) concept of organization led Woodward to reconceptualize management systems into organic and mechanical types, the latter representing the classical type. There are some indications that she was also inclined to identify the organic management system with older types of industrial structures, the mechanical with the more contemporary types, in a manner suggesting the typologies of entire societies by Tönnies and Durkheim. However, the relationships uncovered proved to be somewhat more complex than is suggested by a discussion between older traditional and more recent contemporary industries, with strongest ties appearing between types of technology and types of management system.

The implication this has for both classical management theory and Marxian predictions is obvious. It places classical theory in perspective and aids us in understanding why the dehumanization forseen by Marx never manifested itself in the extreme form he anticipated. It may also be noted that the assertions made by some proponents of the human relations tradition regarding the universal desirability of an organic style appear somewhat dubious in light of these data.

NOTES

1. Classical management theory recognized three types of organizational structure, functional, line, and staff-line. Within this system, however, the staff-line structure was viewed as the optimum form of organization for elaborated organizations.

2. Joan Woodward, *Industrial Organization: Theory and Practice* (London: Oxford University Press, 1965), pp. 23–25.

3. Ferdinand Tönnies, *Fundamental Concepts of Sociology*, trans. Charles P. Loomis (New York: American Book Company, 1940).

4. Émile Durkheim, *The Division of Labor in Society,* trans. George Simpson (New York: The Free Press, 1947).

5. Woodward, *Industrial Organization*, p. 23.

6. It should be noted that this division of management system was not originally Woodward's, being suggested to her by Tom Burns, *Management in the Electronics Industry—A Study of Eight English Companies* (Edinburgh: Social Science Research Center, University of Edinburgh, 1958).

7. Nine of the Minneapolis firms could not be classified as either organic or mechanistic, whether because of the lack of sufficient information or the presence of aspects of both types of systems within a single firm.

8. Woodward, *Industrial Organization,* p. 24.

9. For recent studies, see R. Dubin, "Business Behavior Behaviorally Viewed," *Social Science Approaches to Business Behavior* (Homewood, Ill.: Richard D. Irwin, 1962); R. M. Stodgil and C. L. Shartle, *Methods in the Study of Administrative*

Leadership (Columbus: Bureau of Business Research, Ohio State University, 1955); William E. Henry, "Executive Personality," in *The Emergent American Society,* ed. W. Lloyd Warner (New Haven: Yale University Press, 1967), pp. 241ff.

10. This is the kind of argument presented by Irving Goffman in his analysis of Mental Hospitals, Irving Goffman, *Asylums* (Garden City, New York: Doubleday & Company, 1961).

11. This would be consistent with the identification of *Gemeinschaft* types of communities and relationships with small-scale social units and *Gesellschaft* with large-scale unit.

12. Woodward, *Industrial Organization,* p. 64.

13. This does not distort the data presentation for the same results obtain when finer breaks are made with respect to size of the labor force in the analysis of these variables.

14. While there were too few process firms in the Minneapolis sample to allow for a complete analysis for this type of firm the data in this study are consistent with that presented by Woodward, one of the implications possibly being that increasing technological sophistication may bring with it a return to certain types of organic social systems and types of relationships.

4

ORGANIZATIONAL STRUCTURE

Having failed to account for the success of industrial enterprise in Essex by means of the variables significant in classical organization theory, Woodward appears to have responded by attempting to salvage the classical position. She began by exploring the possibility that the classical organizational formula is produced by a particular combination of technological factors. In Woodward's data and the data of the Minneapolis replication this suggestion seems to bear up. Such corroboration raises the possibility that the general problem of organizational structure and organizational success can most fruitfully be approached from the standpoint of technology.

In the course of its history the significance attributed to technology by analysts has varied. The history of the pendulumlike shifts of interest remains to be written. Perhaps interest in technology and organization have altered as problems of each have remained to be solved. In earlier times, for example, Taylor began his studies with a concern with machines operations, cutting tools and the like, but came, in time, to a concern with work relations. In any case the analysis of data from a technological base forms the climax of Woodward's study.

In her study Woodward summarized the role of technology in ordering her data on the relationship between organizational structure and operating success as follows:

> In the final analysis the conclusions reached earlier had to be modified. While at first sight there seemed to be no link between organization and success, and no one best way of organizing a factory, it subsequently became apparent that there was a particular form of organization most appropriate to each technical situation. Within a limited range of technology this was also the form of organization most closely in line with the principles and ideas of management theory. Outside the limited range, however, the rules appear to be different; the most suitable form of organization being out of line with these principles and ideas.[1]

In her analysis of the form of organization most appropriate to her three general types of industrial technologies,[2] Woodward observed that the four variables—span of control of chief executive, span of control of first-line supervisor, number of levels in the management hierarchy, and relative size of supervisory force—differ in every aspect when unit and small-batch operations were compared with large-batch and mass-production operations. On the other hand, one similarity was observed between unit and small-batch operations and process firms, while process firms were observed to differ on each variable from large-batch and mass-production firms.

The differences observed between unit and small-batch operations, large-batch and mass-production firms, and process firms were most marked when only the very successful firms were compared with one another. This was the primary basis for her conclusion that there are several forms of optimal organization, each specific to a given type of production technology.[3]

To summarize: Woodward found that small-batch and unit operations had narrow spans of control at both the top and the bottom of the organization; they also had short management hierarchies, and a relatively small proportion of supervisory personnel. Their overall structure tended to be short and squat.

Process firms, by contrast, tended to have wide spans of control at the top of the organizational structure and narrow spans at the bottom. They were likely to have tall hierarchies. They also had the greatest ratio of supervisory personnel to production workers. Their structures tended to be tall and narrow.

Large-batch and mass-production firms were likely to have spans of control at the top of the structure which fell between unit and process firms. They had the largest span of control at the level of the first-line supervisor. Their hierarchies were taller than those of unit firms and shorter than those of process firms. They had a greater ratio of supervisory personnel to workers than the unit operations, but fewer than the process firms. With the exception of span of control of first-line supervisor, which was the greatest for the three types of production technology, the values of the variables for large-batch and mass-production firms fell between those of unit and process firms.[4]

All these findings of Woodward suggested that technology was the major clue to industrial organization. It is time to inquire as to the degree to which the Minneapolis data replicated Woodward's finding that technology was the primary factor in the interpretation of organizational structure and operating success.

TECHNOLOGY AND ORGANIZATIONAL STRUCTURE

In the Essex sample the relationship between technology and organizational structure was obvious from an examination of the data applying to all the firms. The control on degree of success merely refined the original findings. In the Minneapolis sample, however, the full extent of the relationship between technology and organizational structure does not appear in the data for all the firms. However, when the successful firms were compared a relationship between technology and organizational structure, quite similar to that found in the English report, also emerged for the Minneapolis data.

In the presentation of the Minneapolis data span of control of both chief executive and first-line supervisors will be examined first, followed by a consideration of the number of levels in the hierarchy and the ratio of nonsupervisory to supervisory personnel.

Span of Control

The concept of "span of control" provided an important structural focus of classical management theory. Explicit concern with this variable dates effectively from the publication of an article by V. A. Graicunas, "Relationship in Organization," in 1933.[5] Graicunas advanced the hypothesis that no man (brain) could adequately supervise the activities of more than six other men (brains). On the other hand, supervision of fewer than three others represented less than a full-time investment of energy. The optimum span of control defined, then, was from three to six, with Graicunas arguing that the optimum span decreased as one approached the apex, narrowing down to three, and increased as one moved toward the bottom of the structure, approaching six.

Classical management theorists immediately reacted to the specific numbers proposed by Graicunas. Gulick suggested that factors such as the repetitiveness and routine of the work, along with the need for coordination of activity, were determinates of the actual desired span of control. Gulick went on to suggest that at the lower levels one supervisor could conceivably supervise several scores of workers under optimal conditions, while a smaller number would be desirable at the top, the number 10–12 being suggested in certain circumstances.[6]

But while there was a reaction to the specifics of Graicunas' argument there was a general acceptance of the importance of the concept of "span of control" which forthwith became one of the structural focuses of organizational analysis in this tradition.

In his 1937 statement Gulick urged: "But when we seek to determine how many immediate subordinates the director of an enterprise can effectively supervise, we enter a realm of experience which has not been brought under sufficient scientific study to furnish a final answer."[7] That this evaluation of the empirical state of affairs of 1937 is still relevant is indicated by Simon's reference to the notion of limited span as a "proverb of administration"[8] and Udell's recent comment that "surprisingly little research has been conducted on the subject." While Woodward's analysis does not yield a final answer to this question, it does provide a significant beginning of the empirical analysis of the concept of span of control in the context of organizational theory.

Woodward's findings are particularly clear on this point, for she discovers two different patterns of relationship between technological complexity and span of control. In the case of span of control of chief executive, she notes that this increases with increasing technological complexity, being a direct function of technology, while for span of control of first-line supervisor she finds that unit and process firms are similar in manifesting narrow spans of control at this level, whereas mass-production firms manifest the broadest spans of control at the bottom of the organization.[9]

The isolation of these two different patterns of relationship between technology and span of control clearly precludes the possibility that the managers of the firms studied were committed to any of the notions currently promulgated regarding span of control.[10]

The Minneapolis Findings

Beginning with span of control of chief executive, the primary concern of classical management theory, the Minneapolis data support Woodward's argument that the optimum span of control of chief executive increases with increasing technological complexity. The data for the Minneapolis sample and that available for the English study are presented in Table 8.

The ranges in span of control for the Minneapolis and Essex firms were comparable. The only notable exception was the somewhat greater range of the process firms in the Essex sample. The medians for the firms move in the same direction, increasing with increasing technological complexity. However, the dispersion of medians was somewhat greater for the English firms: In the Minneapolis sample the range for unit firms is 1–9, with a median of 5, compared with a range of 2–9 and a median of 4 for the English sample. For large-batch and mass-production firms the range for the Minneapolis sample was 3–15, with a median of 6, compared with a range of 4–13 and a median of 7 for the English firms. In the case of process firms the range for the Minneapolis sample was 4–14 with a median of 8.5, compared with a range of 5–19 and a median of 10 for the English sample.

TABLE 8

PRODUCTION TECHNOLOGY, SPAN OF CONTROL OF CHIEF EXECUTIVE, AND LEVEL OF BUSINESS SUCCESS IN MINNEAPOLIS AND ENGLISH FIRMS

SPAN OF CONTROL AND LEVEL OF SUCCESS	TECHNOLOGY					
	Unit and Small-Batch		Mass		Process	
	No.	%	No.	%	No.	%
All Minneapolis Firms						
1–3	3	17	3	11	—	—
4–5	7	39	10	36	1	17
6–7	5	28	9	32	1	17
8–10	3	17	4	14	2	33
11 or more	—	—	2	7	2	33
Total	18	101	28	100	6	100
Median	5		6		8.5	
No information	1		2		—	
All English Firms						
Range	2–9		4–13		5–19	
Median	4		7		10	
Very Successful Minneapolis Firms						
1–3	2	22	1	8	—	—
4–5	5	56	2	15	1	17
6–7	1	11	6	46	1	17
8–10	1	11	2	15	2	33
11 or more	—	—	2	15	2	33
Total	9	100	13	99	6	100
Median	4		6		8.5	
No information	1		2		—	

When only the very successful Minneapolis firms were examined the differences in span of control of chief executive which were associated with production technology were greater than for the sample as a whole. For the very successful firms the Minneapolis median for unit and small-batch operations was 4 compared to 6 for the mass-production operations and 8.5 for the process firms.

These findings support Woodward's argument that direct links are observable between production technology and organizational structure and, furthermore, the refinement of differences observed when comparing only the very successful firms supports her argument that there is no single optimum form of organization but rather several optimum forms, each specific to a given technology.

It may be noted in passing that the spans of control for process firms show every indication of falling well beyond the range of acceptability as this is defined in the classical management literature.

While span of control of chief executive was the primary concern of classical management theory, span of control at the bottom was also of some interest. In the English study, span of control of first-line supervisors proved to be the variable most strongly linked to production technology. This was, in fact, the only variable of which Woodward gave a complete accounting. She demonstrated that variation in span of control of first-line supervisor was associated with general type of production system,[11] with each level of technological complexity,[12] and there were variations between firms of each type of technology according to degree of success of the operation.[13]

In the English sample of unit operations first-line span

of control ranged from less than 10 to 60, with a median of 23. The range for mass-product on operations was 11–90, with a median of 49. The range for process operations was from less than 10 to 40, with a median of 13. The ranges for the very successful firms were much smaller and clustered about the median value for each of the three major types of production systems.[14] The average number of persons controlled by the supervisor increased from the simplest form of production system—the manufacture of items to customer specification—through the mass-production stage, then dropped sharply when the process stage of production was reached. In the case of unit-production firms the averages varied from 14 for Type I production technologies, production of units to customers' special requirements to, 20 for Type II, 27 for Type III and 30 for Type IV, the production of small batches; the average span of control continued to rise through the three types of large-batch and mass-production firms, 37 for Type V, the production of large batches, 44 for Type VI, and 56 for Type VII, mass production: the average of span of control of first-line supervisors then dropped sharply for the two types of process industries, down to 18 for Type VIII and 11 for Type IX.[15]

Such striking differences were not found in the Minneapolis sample. Indeed, no differences were observed in the Minneapolis sample with respect to the span of control of first-line supervisors as between the various types of production systems (Appendix 3, Table 29).

In the Minneapolis sample the median span of control of first-line supervisors in unit and small-batch operations was 20.0; in large-batch and mass-production firms it was 19.8, and in process firms it was 16.8. For the very successful Minneapolis firms the median span of control of supervisors for the unit, mass, and process firms were 19, 20, and 16.8 respectively. The relationship between production technology and span of control of first-line supervisor in the Minneapolis sample did not correspond to Woodward's findings in the Essex sample.

Ratio of Supervisory Personnel

The ratio of managers and supervisors to nonsupervisory personnel is normally related to the span of control in a firm. Woodward found a direct relationship between the relative size of the firm's supervisory group and technological complexity. In the English sample it was observed that the median number of nonsupervisory persons for each supervisor was 23 for unit and small-batch production, 16 for large-batch and mass-production, and 8 for process-production firms.[16] In the Minneapolis sample the relative proportion of supervisors is greater for the sample as a whole. (See pages 38–39 and Appendix 3, Table 35.) This need not have any bearing on the predicted relationship between technology and this organizational variable.

The data for the Minneapolis sample (see Table 9), supported Woodward's initial finding. While the ranges of this variable were essentially the same for the three types of production systems, the median values differed considerably in the predicted direction. The median ratio of nonsupervisory to supervisory personnel was 12 for unit and small-batch firms, 10.5 for large-batch and mass-production firms, and 5 for process operations.

TABLE 9

PRODUCTION TECHNOLOGY, RATIO OF NONSUPERVISORY TO SUPERVISORY PERSONNEL, AND LEVEL OF BUSINESS SUCCESS IN MINNEAPOLIS AND ENGLISH FIRMS

RATIO OF NON-SUPERVISORY TO SUPERVISORY PERSONNEL AND LEVEL OF SUCCESS	TECHNOLOGY					
	Unit and Small-Batch		Mass		Process	
	No.	%	No.	%	No.	%
All Minneapolis Firms						
1–6	1	5	10	36	4	80
7–12	9	47	5	18	1	20
13–18	5	26	8	29	—	—
19 or more	4	21	5	18	—	—
Total	19	99	28	101	5	100
Median	12		10.5		5	
No information	—		2		1	
All English Firms						
Median	23		16		8	
Very Successful Minneapolis Firms						
1–6	1	10	6	46	4	80
7–12	5	50	2	15	1	20
13–18	1	10	2	15	—	—
19 or more	3	30	3	23	—	—
Total	10	100	13	99	5	100
Median	11.5		9		5	
No information	—		2		1	

The differences between the types of production systems were clearer when only the very successful firms were compared with one another; the median for very successful unit and small-batch operations being 11.5, compared with 9 for equally successful large-batch and mass-production firms and 5 for process firms.

The ratios of nonsupervisory to supervisory personnel observed in the Minneapolis data not only supported the original Essex finding of a link between technology and organization, but once again supported Woodward's argument regarding the need to view optimal organization as specific to particular types of organizational technology.

Levels of Management

The number of levels in a supervisory hierarchy is related to the span of control in a given organization, and the relative preponderance of supervisors is correlated with this hierarchical variable.

Woodward observed that the number of levels of management in a firm, the number intervening between the production worker and the board, varied directly with increasing technological complexity. In the Essex sample it was observed that the median number of levels of management for unit operations was 3, compared to 4 for large-batch and mass-production systems and 6 for process firms.[17]

The Minneapolis data once again supported Woodward's findings, as shown in Table 10.

The median number of management levels for Minneapolis unit and small-batch firms was 4 compared with 5 for the large-batch and mass-production firms and 6 for process

TABLE 10

PRODUCTION TECHNOLOGY, NUMBER OF LEVELS OF MANAGEMENT, AND LEVEL OF BUSINESS SUCCESS IN MINNEAPOLIS AND ENGLISH FIRMS

NUMBER OF LEVELS OF MANAGEMENT AND LEVEL OF SUCCESS	TECHNOLOGY					
	Unit and Small-Batch		Mass		Process	
	No.	%	No.	%	No.	%
All Minneapolis Firms						
2–3	8	44	1	3	—	—
4	3	17	9	30	—	—
5	5	28	9	30	1	17
6 or more	2	11	11	37	5	83
Total	18	100	30	100	6	100
Median	4		5		6	
No information	1		—		—	
All English Firms						
2–3	11	79	2	6	—	—
4	3	21	16	52	2	8
5	—	—	7	23	6	24
6 or more	—	—	6	19	17	68
Total	14	100	31	100	25	100
Median	3		4		6	
Very Successful Minneapolis Firms						
2–3	4	44	—	—	—	—
4	2	22	3	20	—	—
5	3	33	5	33	1	17
6 or more	—	—	7	47	5	83
Total	9	99	15	100	6	100
Median	4		5		6	
No information	1		—		—	

Organizational Structure

operations. These medians are very similar to the 3, 4, and 6 reported by Woodward. The major difference between the two sets of firms was the somewhat greater range of values present among unit and small-batch operations in the Minneapolis sample.

As in span of control of chief executive and ratio of nonsupervisory to supervisory personnel, the differences observed among the Minneapolis firms were greatest between the most successful operations.

So far Woodward's findings are strongly supported by the Minneapolis data. With the exception of the posited relationship between technology and span of control of first-line supervisors, each of the relationships examined in the replication has supported Woodward's original findings.

However, the possible effect of two other factors, size of labor force and separation of ownership and management, must be considered. The lack of variation with respect to span of control of first-line supervisors strongly suggests the possibility that the mechanical relationship between span of control and number of levels in the hierarchy may produce a correlation between size of labor force and number of levels, independent of the effect of technology. Furthermore, the separation of ownership and management could also be a consideration—for owner-managers, out of concern for personal control, could be inclined to keep the number of levels in the hierarchy to a minimum in their firms. In this case the number of competing supervisory personnel would be kept down, and the span of control at the top would be severely limited in the interest of maintaining personal control of the organization.

SIZE OF LABOR FORCE AND ORGANIZATIONAL STRUCTURE

When the relation between size of labor force and structural characteristics of the organizations was examined, two general findings appeared. First, when differences related to size were observed there was generally little divergence in either the range of values of the organizational variables or the median values observed. Secondly, in each case where differences were observed between firms of different sizes they were either attenuated when only the very successful firms were compared with one another—suggesting that something other than rational organizational construction is at work—or (in one case) they were reversed.

Span of Control

Span of control of chief executive is closely linked to size of labor force. Indeed, it is the only one of the four structural variables showing a strong correlation with this index of organizational size.

The data bearing on the relationship between size of labor force and span of control of chief executive are presented in Table 11, where it may be observed that the range of span of control for organizations with 1,000 or fewer employees was 1–11, with a median of 4.5, while the range of values for organizations with greater than 1,000 employees was 5–15, with a median of 7. A comparison of the very successful firms, varying with respect to size, revealed that the difference in range was modestly attenuated over that observed for the sample as a whole, 2–11 for the smaller firms compared to 5–15 for the larger ones, and that the medians were slightly less divergent when only the very successful firms were compared—5 for the smaller firms and 7 for the larger ones.

While there was no refinement of the relationship observed when only the very successful firms were compared, the differences observed in this instance were certainly great enough to suggest the possibility that size of labor force may be directly related to span of control of chief executive, independently of any relationship between span of control of chief executive and other variables. The interaction of technology and size of labor force in this respect is examined later in this section of the analysis.

The other measure of span of control, that of the first-line supervisor, was not related to size of labor force among the firms in the sample. The median span of control of first-line supervisor for all firms with 1,000 or fewer employees was 20, compared to 18.3 for the firms with greater than 1,000 employees. In the case of the very successful firms the median span for the smaller firms was 20, while that of the larger firms was 23.5 (Appendix 3, Table 30).

With respect to span of control, then, there does appear to be a possible relationship between size of labor force and span of control of chief executive, although this relationship was not perceivably related to operating success, per se. No relationship was observed between span of control of first-line supervisor and size of labor force.

TABLE 11

SIZE OF LABOR FORCE, SPAN OF CONTROL OF CHIEF EXECUTIVE, AND LEVEL OF BUSINESS SUCCESS IN MINNEAPOLIS FIRMS

SPAN OF CONTROL AND LEVEL OF SUCCESS	SIZE OF LABOR FORCE			
	1,000 or less[a]		More than 1,000	
	No.	%	No.	%
All Firms				
1–3	6	18	—	—
4–5	14	41	4	22
6–7	9	26	6	33
8–10	4	12	5	28
11 or more	1	3	3	17
Total	34	100	18	100
Median	4.5		7	
No information	1		2	
Very Successful Firms				
1–3	3	19	—	—
4–5	5	31	3	23
6–7	5	31	4	31
8–10	2	12	3	23
11 or more	1	6	3	23
Total	16	99	13	100
Median	5		7	
No information	—		2	

[a] The division of the firms into those with 1,000 or fewer employees and those with greater than 1,000 employees does not distort the analysis; finer differences with respect to differences in the size of the labor force do not strengthen or weaken the observed relationship in any way relevant to this analysis.

Ratio of Supervisory Personnel

The Minneapolis data on the relationship between size of labor force and ratio of nonsupervisory to supervisory personnel was quite consistent with the literature on the relationship between size of organization and relative size of administrative unit—inconclusive and inconsistent.[18]

For the sample as a whole the range for firms with 1,000 or fewer employees is 3 to greater than 20, with a median of 11 nonsupervisory workers to one supervisor; for firms with greater than 1,000 employees the range is one to greater than 20, with a median of 9. For the sample as a whole, then, the ranges are comparable for the different size firms but the median ratio of nonsupervisory to supervisory personnel is somewhat lower for the larger firms. When only the very successful firms are considered the ranges for the larger and smaller firms are once again comparable, but now it is found the ratio for the smaller firms is somewhat lower than that of the larger—an average of 8 nonsupervisory persons to one supervisor for the smaller firms compared with 10.5 for the larger firms (Appendix 3, Table 31).

The data at hand bearing on the relationship between size of labor force and relative size of supervisory group suggest no relationship between these two variables.

Levels of Management

The final structural variable to be considered is the number of levels of management. Woodward's report of finding no association between these two variables is supported by the recent publication of Hall, Haas, and Johnson,[19] where no significant differences are reported between firms with 100–999 employees and those with 1,000 or more with respect to the range of number of levels and the median number of levels in the firms.

TABLE 12

SIZE OF LABOR FORCE, NUMBER OF LEVELS OF MANAGEMENT, AND LEVEL OF BUSINESS SUCCESS IN MINNEAPOLIS FIRMS

NUMBER OF LEVELS OF MANAGEMENT AND LEVEL OF SUCCESS	SIZE OF LABOR FORCE			
	1,000 or less		More than 1,000	
	No.	%	No.	%
All Firms				
2–3	9	26	—	—
4	10	29	2	11
5	8	23	7	37
6 or more	8	23	10	53
Total	35	101	19	101
Median	4		6	
No information	—		1	
Very Successful Firms				
2–3	4	25	—	—
4	4	25	1	7
5	3	19	6	43
6 or more	5	31	7	50
Total	16	100	14	100
Median	4.5		5.5	
No information	—		—	

In the Minneapolis data a difference was observed for the total sample of larger and smaller firms, but this difference was considerably attenuated when only the very successful firms were compared with one another (Table 12).

When all of the larger and smaller firms were compared with respect to the number of management levels in the organizations, a difference in both range and median number of levels was observed. The smaller firms had a range of 3–6 levels with a median of 4, compared with a range of 4–8 levels and a median of 6 for the larger firms.

When only the very successful firms were compared with one another both the ranges and the median number of levels of the different-sized firms were more comparable to one another than is true for the sample as a whole; the range was 3–6, with a median of 4.5 for the smaller firms, while the larger firms had a range of 4–7, with a median of 5.5.

The differences observed with respect to size of the labor force and number of management levels suggests that a simple correlation between size and length of the hierarchy may be found, but there is not much support for arguing that this is also related to organization success.

It is precisely the multiple link observed among type of production system, number of levels in the hierarchy, and the relationship of these factors to operating success that provides the strongest support for the posited relationship between technology and this organizational characteristic.

Review

Of the four structural variables considered only one, span of control of chief executive, showed a strong relationship to size of labor force, but even in this case the relationship was slightly weakened when only the successful operations were compared with another.

Number of levels in the management hierarchy is related to size of labor force for the total sample, but the meaning and importance of the relationship is seriously challenged by the attenuation of the correlation observed when only the successful firms were compared with one another.

The ratio of nonsupervisory personnel to supervisors and span of control of first-line supervisor were not found to be related to size of labor force.

At this point in the analysis Woodward's argument for the primacy of production technology, over size of labor force, as a determinate of organizational characteristics is still supported. The variances observed here with respect to strength of relationships between technology and structural characteristics, and the suggestions of one possibly rather strong relationship between size of labor force and one organizational characteristics, are important and are dealt with later.

SEPARATION OF OWNERSHIP AND MANAGEMENT AND ORGANIZATIONAL STRUCTURE

As pointed out previously, the effect of separation of ownership and management was not considered in the Essex study if only for the reason that there were no examples of combined ownership and management present.

The primary consideration which dictated the hypothesized relationships between separation of ownership and management and structural characteristics is the assumption that one of the primary goals of the owner-manager is the desire for personal control of the organization. Assuming that extensive personal control is of importance to the owner-manager, we would predict that he would attempt to minimize span of control, particularly at the top of the organization, in order to maximize knowledge and control of the activities of his subordinates; that he would attempt to minimize the relative size of the supervisory force in order to minimize intraorganizational challenges to his control; and that he would attempt to maintain a short managerial hierarchy in order to remain close to all phases of the organizations operations.

Span of Control

The predicted relationship was found in span of control of chief executive, but not in span of control of first-line supervisor.

For firms with combined ownership and management the range of span of control of chief executive was 3–11 with a median of 4, compared with a range of 1–15 with a median of 6 for firms with separated ownership and management. This difference was maintained when only the very successful firms are compared with one another (Table 13).

Span of control of first-line supervisor was not correlated with the separation of ownership and management.

TABLE 13

SEPARATION OF OWNERSHIP AND MANAGEMENT, SPAN OF CONTROL OF CHIEF EXECUTIVE, AND LEVEL OF BUSINESS SUCCESS IN MINNEAPOLIS FIRMS

SPAN OF CONTROL AND LEVEL OF SUCCESS	OWNERSHIP AND MANAGEMENT			
	Combined		Separated	
	No.	%	No.	%
All Firms				
1–3	3	19	3	8
4–5	7	44	11	31
6–7	4	25	11	31
8–10	1	6	8	22
11 or more	1	6	3	8
Total	16	100	36	100
Median	4		6	
No information	—		3	
Very Successful Firms				
1–3	1	17	2	9
4–5	3	50	5	23
6–7	1	17	7	32
8–10	—	—	5	23
11 or more	1	17	3	14
Total	6	101	22	101
Median	4		6	
No information	—		3	

For the sample as a whole the median number of persons supervised at the first level of the organization was 20 for those firms with combined ownership and management, and

19.3 for those with separated ownership and management. For the very successful firms the median was 18.4 for those with combined ownership and management and 19.5 for those with separated ownership and management (Appendix 3, Table 32).

Ratio of Supervisors

It was predicted that the ratio of nonsupervisory personnel to supervisors would be greater for firms with combined ownership and management than for firms where these are separated.

The Minneapolis data provided partial support for this hypothesis. The ranges for the firms were the same, whether there was a combination or separation of ownership and management, but the medians for the total sample differ, the median for the combined firms being 12 and that for the separated firms 9. This relationship is called into question, however, by the observation that the medians for the very successful firms were identical, 8.5. Thus while there was a gross difference observed for the two types of firms this was not related to operating success and does not occupy the same position in the analysis as does the relationship between production technology and the ratio of nonsupervisory personnel to supervisors (Appendix 3, Table 33).

Levels of Management

It was hypothesized that the owner-manager's desire for control of the organization would lead him to minimize the length of the supervisory hierarchy. The Minneapolis data support this hypothesis (Table 14).

TABLE 14

SEPARATION OF OWNERSHIP AND MANAGEMENT, NUMBER OF LEVELS OF MANAGEMENT, AND LEVEL OF BUSINESS SUCCESS IN MINNEAPOLIS FIRMS

NUMBER OF LEVELS OF MANAGEMENT AND LEVEL OF SUCCESS	OWNERSHIP AND MANAGEMENT			
	Combined		Separated	
	No.	%	No.	%
All Firms				
2–3	6	38	3	8
4	5	31	7	18
5	3	19	12	32
6 or more	2	12	16	42
Total	16	100	38	100
Median	4		5	
No information	—		1	
Very Successful Firms				
2–3	3	50	1	4
4	2	33	3	12
5	1	17	8	33
6 or more	—	—	12	50
Total	6	100	24	99
Median	3.5		5.5	
No information	—		1	

In Table 14 it can be seen the range for all combined firms was 3–6 with a median of 4, compared with a range of 3–8 with a median of 5 for the firms with separation of ownership and management. Furthermore, this difference increased when only the very successful firms are compared with one another, the range for the very successful combined firms being 3–5 with a median of 3.5, compared with a range of 3–7 with a median of 5.5 where there was separation.

Review

The separation of ownership and management did appear to be related to span of control of chief executive and number of levels in the management hierarchy.

There remains, then, an examination of the interaction of production technology, size of labor force, and separation of ownership and management as they affect these structural characteristics of the organization.

INTERACTION OF THE INDEPENDENT VARIABLE WITH THE STRUCTURAL CHARACTERISTICS

A complete analysis of the interaction of the proposed independent variables, production technology, size of labor force, and separation of ownership and management is impossible. First, there are no firms in the Minneapolis sample with labor forces greater than 1,000 which are controlled by owner-managers. Secondly, the size of the sample, 55, is too small to allow for a complex analysis of the relationships of five variables, the three independent variables, a single structural characteristic, and operating success.

What may be investigated is the relationship between production technology and each of the other two independent variables—at least to a limited extent.

The structural characteristics to be considered are span of control of the chief executive and number of levels in the management hierarchy, the variables which appeared that they might be related to all three of the independent variables.

Span of Control of Chief Executive

The effect of combined ownership and management was visible even when looking only at firms with the same type of production technology. The numbers involved in this portion of the analysis are quite small but are all consistent.

For the sixteen firms with combined ownership and management, span of control of chief executive did not vary a great deal with type of production technology, the median value being 4 for unit and small-batch firms ($n = 9$), 4.5 for large-batch and mass-production operations ($n = 6$), and the single-process firms with combined ownership and management had an executive span of control of 4.

In the case of those firms with separated ownership and management, span of control of chief executive did vary with respect to type of production technology, the median value being 5 for the unit and small-batch operations ($n = 9$), 6 for the large-batch and mass-production firms ($n = 22$), 9 for the process technologies ($n = 5$).

The relationship between size of labor force and production technology, with respect to span of control of chief executive suggested that the two variables may interact in influencing span of control of chief executive within a firm. For the smaller firms the median spans of control of chief executive were 4 for unit, 5 for mass, and 6 for process firms. For the larger firms the median spans of control were 7 for unit, 6 for mass, and 13 for process operations. (The presence of only four large-unit and small-batch operations makes an interpretation impossible at this point of the rather large median span of control of the chief executive, 7.)

The general pattern with respect to span of control of chief executive appears to be, first, that the variations observed by Woodward which were associated with type of production system may be specific to firms which have undergone separation of ownership and management. Secondly, within the class of firms operating with separated ownership and management, both types of production system and size of labor force may affect this variable. The extent of this complex relationship and its relationship to operating success is beyond the limits of analysis of this data.

Levels of Management

The relationship between number of levels of management and the independent variables appears to be as complex as that relating to span of control of chief executive.

When the relationship between type of production technology, size of labor force and number of levels of management was examined, it was observed that the median number of levels within categories varies both with respect to type of technology and size of labor force. The median number of levels for smaller firms is 3 for unit, 4.5 for mass, and 6 for process operations. In the case of the larger firms, the medians were 5 for unit, 5.5 for mass, and 7 for process operations. Thus within given types of production systems, size appeared to be related to number of levels of management, the median number of levels for small-unit operations was 3 compared with 5 for their larger counterparts. The median was 4.5 among smaller mass operations compared with 5.5 for the large operations, and among process firms the median was 6 for the smaller operations and 7 for the larger ones.

In similar fashion, the relationship between production technology and separation of ownership and management appeared to have an interactive effect on number of levels in the hierarchy. The relationship here was rather difficult to interpret, and it is regrettable that the sample was not larger with a representation of large firms with combined ownership and management. What was observed in this instance is that unit and small-batch operations with combined ownership and management had very short hierarchies, with a median of 3. The process operations with separated ownership and management had rather long hierarchies, median of 7, and that all of the other subtypes had roughly equivalent hierarchies.

Unit and mass-production firms with separated ownership and management have the same median number of levels of management, 5. Unit and mass-production firms with combined ownership and management had similar median numbers of levels of management, 3 and 4 respectively, and roughly the same range of values.

An examination, to the extent possible, of the relative importance of production technology, size of labor force, and separation of ownership and management as predictors of two structural characteristics of manufacturing operations—span of control of chief executive and number of levels in management hierarchy—suggested that these factors may operate independently of one another in affecting the formal structural characteristics of manufacturing organizations. Insofar as Woodward's original findings are concerned, there were no data presented to challenge her assertion of the importance of production technology as a determinate of these two structural variables. Our data suggest that technology may interact with size and organizational control in this determinate relationship. The data were insufficient to allow for a thorough examination of these complex relationships and did not permit any meaningful analysis of the relationship between the factors and operating success.

SUMMARY

The analysis of the relationship between production technology and the structural characteristics of the Minneapolis manufacturing firms was supportive of Woodward's original findings. Span of control of chief executive, ratio of nonsupervisionist to supervisory personnel, and number of levels in management hierarchy were found to vary directly with increasing technological complexity. The differences observed were greatest when only the very successful firms were compared with one another.

The single exception to Woodward's findings involved

span of control of first-line supervisor which did not vary with respect to type of production technology. In fact this was a variable that was not related to any of the proposed independent variables.

In the case of ratio of supervisory personnel to production workers, technology was the only independent variable that accounted for variation in this variable.

Span of control of chief executive and number of levels in management hierarchy appeared to be related, to one extent or another, to all three of the independent variables. The relationship between these two structural characteristics was most clearly connected with production technology, the patterning of the range of values being most differentiated in this case, and the link between variations in these variables and success being observed only in the analysis of production technology.

At this point in the analysis it appears as though elements of both the Marxian and classical analyses are relevant to an understanding of the data from the Essex and Minneapolis study.

In the case of Marxian analysis, both the perspective of materialistic determinism and the theory of exploitation are consistent with some of the data, particularly that related to the two forms of production known to Marx: unit and small batch, and mass production. The general relationship between style of management and structural characteristics to the forms of production technology supports Marx's emphasis upon the importance of material factors as conditioners of social life. The relationship observed between the owner-manager firms and structural characteristics also supports his contention that the goals of the entrepreneurial capitalist are control of the production facility and of the men and women working within it.

On the other hand, the association between an organic form of management and process production, as well as the growing importance of separation of ownership and management is more consistent with the classical perspective which emphasized managerial rationality rather than worker exploitation. In this case it would appear that the new forms of production dictate a looser and more participative form of organization, as indicated by the data on style of management and by the preponderance of supervisors in process firms.

Thus, so far, the Marxian analysis is consistent with the data on owner-manager firms utilizing unit or mass production technologies. The Marxian perspective is also consistent with the observed importance of technology. It is not, however, so consistent with the data on process firms or on firms with separated ownership and management.

NOTES

1. Joan Woodward, *Industrial Organization: Theory and Practice* (London: Oxford University Press, 1965), p. 72.

2. It should be noted explicitly that while Woodward developed the scale of technology, specifying nine stages in the development of increasingly complex production technologies, she centered her empirical analysis on the three general types of production technology which have been and will continue to be utilized in this replication.

3. Woodward, *Industrial Organization,* pp. 68–72.

4. Ibid., pp. 52–53, 55, 57, 60, 62, 69, 71.

5. V. A. Graicunas, "Relationship in Organization," reprinted in *Papers on the Science of Administration* ed. Luther Gulick and L. Urwick (New York: Institute of Public Administration, Columbia University, 1937), pp. 181–187.

6. Gulick, "Notes on the Theory of Organization" in *Papers on the Science of Administration,* Gulick and Urwick, pp. 7–9.

7. Ibid., p. 8.

8. Herbert A. Simon, *Administrative Behavior* (New York: The Free Press, 1965), p. 26; and Jon G. Udell, "An Empirical Test of Hypotheses Relating to Span of Control," *Administrative Science Quarterly* 12 (December, 1967): 420–439, esp. p. 421. Udell does not consider any of the independent variables being investigated here in his study.

9. Considerations arising from the fact that Woodward's types do not form a true scale are deferred for the moment.

10. Recently the notion has been advanced that broad spans of control are inherently desirable and related to productivity and operational success. See, for example, James C. Worthy, "Factors Influencing Employees Morale," *Harvard Business Review* 28 (January, 1950): 61–73.

11. Woodward, *Industrial Organization,* p. 62.

12. Ibid., p. 61.

13. Ibid., pp. 69–70.

14. Ibid., p. 69.

15. Ibid., p. 61.

16. Ibid., p. 55.

17. Ibid., p. 52.

18. For a general summary and evaluation of the work in this area, see Richard H. Hall, J. Eugene Haas, and Norman J. Johnson, "Organizational Size and Organizational Structure," *American Sociological Review* 32 (December, 1967):903–912.

19. Ibid., p. 909.

5

TECHNOLOGY AND LABOR

Woodward's attempt to combine the classical economic and Marxian approaches with organizational analysis into a single perspective has some historical justification. Both the classical economists and the Marxians addressed themselves to the same industrial complex—emerging English mass production. Marx accepted as unquestioned many features of the classical explanation of the operation of the English economic system—the role of the market, the importance and effect of the division of labor and specialization, the notion of the economic rationality of man, and so forth. Marx, in short, did not begin his analysis with a rejection of the classical economic analysis. He accepted it and made it the foundation for new emphasis and interpretation.

Traditions that branch from a common stock may diverge in time, and so it was with the classical economic and Marxian interpretations of socioeconomic life. As time passed exponents of each tended to emphasize the difference of his position from the other. Classical economics and Marxism had begun to acquire the properties of ideologies in the power operations of social groups—classical economics for business groups, Marxism for labor groups. Carried to its conclusion, this process leads to the tendency by exponents of one position to reject in principle everything distinctive about the other.

As the two positions continued to develop in polemical opposition, each tended to emphasize factors strategically important to its respective bearer: classical economics emphasized the entrepreneurs operations (management) and the conditions of his operation (the market); Marxian economics emphasized the means (technology) and relations (labor) of production. To be sure, each position took account of the variables central to the other (as is to be expected, since the two positions diverged from a common matrix), but tended to play them down and move them from the center of analysis.

Now there is no question that Woodward's point of departure in her original analysis was classical economic theory, for the variables she initially took as crucial in her survey of the industrial establishments of southeast Essex were the structure of management and success in the marketplace. When her initial study came to grief, Woodward immediately set to work to salvage from the disaster what she was able of the classical position on organization.

However, the full drama of Woodward's study and the clearest evidence of her soundness as a social scientist appears only when one follows her struggles to rethink the whole tradition of organizational analysis and her attempts to tear both the classical economic and Marxian analyses out of their ideological wrappings in order to deal anew with the variables. Hence after salvaging what she was able of the classical economic conception of organization, Woodward turned her attention to what the Marxians would describe as the means of production (technology) as a possible class of variables directly associated with effective industrial organization and industrial success.

Our replication has followed Woodward's procedure step-by-step: the attempt to account for industrial organizational success by the classical position (Chapter 2); the attempt to salvage the classical approach to organization (Chapter 3); the attempt to account for successful industrial operations on the basis of technology (Chapter 4). By and large the replication has confirmed Woodward at each phase.

If one tentatively accepts the conclusion to which all this appears to lead—that it is time to rethink both the classical economic and Marxian positions—then the next logical group of variables to examine are those which in Marxian analysis were conceived as "relations of production," in particular, labor. It may be noted that Woodward had begun to move along this line.

TECHNOLOGY AND LABOR

Woodward observed several interesting relationships between production technology and labor, among these being a relationship between technology and the ratio of direct to indirect labor, the promotion policy of the firms, and proportionate labor costs.

In addition to these three variables, the replication will consider the ratio of managers to other supervisory personnel, a variable not included in Woodward's analysis but one relevant to the relationship between the two organizational perspectives.

Ratio of Production to Nonproduction Workers

In the Essex study, data on the ratio of direct to indirect workers was reported, the number decreasing with technological complexity. In the replication, data are presented on the ratio of production to nonproduction workers, this being a somewhat less ambiguous dichotomy of workers and one more closely related to the focus of concern of the analysis, production technology.

In the replication, the findings of the English study receive only partial confirmation (Table 15). It may be observed that for the sample as a whole the ratio of production to nonproduction workers is smallest for the process firms (median = 0.56), and largest for the unit firms (median = 3), with the mass-production operations falling somewhat in between (median = 2). However, when only the very successful firms are compared with one another the median values are 0.56 for the process operations, 3 for the mass-production firms, and only 2 for the unit and small-batch operations.

In the case of the Minneapolis firms, the process operations showed a considerably lower ratio of production to nonproduction workers than was true of the others. The difference between the unit and mass-production firms observed in the English study were not found here. The rather low ratio of production to nonproduction workers observed in the American sample is quite consistent with the relatively higher proportion of supervisors found in the American firms, since for a given number of production workers the ratio is partially determined by the number of supervisors in the firm.

One technological factor commented upon by Woodward as affecting the proportion of direct to indirect workers was also observed in the Minneapolis sample—namely, the complexity of the product in unit and small-batch operations. Woodward observed that "The firms making technically complex products, both prototypes or large equipments, had a higher ratio of clerical and administrative staff to hourly-paid than those making simple products to customers' individual requirements, either as unit articles or in small batches."[1]

In the Minneapolis sample four out of the five very successful unit and small-batch firms, with ratios of one or less, engaged in the manufacture of very complex products. The median ratio of the very successful unit operations, manufacturing very complex items, was one compared with

TABLE 15

PRODUCTION TECHNOLOGY, RATIO OF PRODUCTION TO NONPRODUCTION WORKERS, AND LEVEL OF BUSINESS SUCCESS IN MINNEAPOLIS AND ESSEX FIRMS

RATIO OF PRODUCTION TO NONPRODUCTION WORKERS AND LEVEL OF SUCCESS	TECHNOLOGY					
	Small-Batch Unit and		Mass		Process	
	No.	%	No.	%	No.	%
All Minneapolis Firms						
1 or less	5	26	4	13	5	83
2–3	6	32	16	53	1	17
4–5	5	26	5	17	—	—
6 or more	3	16	5	17	—	—
Total	19	100	30	100	6	100
Median	3		2		0.56	
All Essex Firms						
1 or less	—	—	—	—	20	87
2–3	3	12	13	46	3	13
4–5	1	4	10	36	—	—
6 or more	20	83	5	18	—	—
Total	24	99	28	100	23	100
Median	9		4		1	
Very Successful Minneapolis Firms						
1 or less	5	50	2	13	5	87
2–3	3	30	8	53	1	13
4–5	2	20	2	13	—	—
6 or more	—	—	3	20	—	—
Total	10	100	15	99	6	100
Median	1.5		3		0.56	

four for those engaged in the production of technologically simple items. No such relationship between complexity of the product and ratio of production to nonproduction workers was observed in mass-production and process manufacturing.

The replication provides tentative support for the relationship observed between the ratio of production to nonproduction workers and technology as found in the Essex study.

Ratio of Supervisors to Managers

Among nonproduction employees (administrative staff) of the industrial concern the relation between manager and supervisor is subject to variation. One of Woodward's major findings, supported in the present analysis,[2] was that the overall style of management of manufacturing firms varied with the type of production technology. Unit and process firms often possessed relatively loose and flexible organization structures and organic styles, while mass-production operations were likely to have relatively rigid and formalized patterns of organization and mechanical styles.

It is hypothesized that a mechanical management style most easily arises in an organizational setting where work tasks are highly routinized and simplified. In Dubin's terms,[3] mechanical styles are associated with task subdivision:

> Subdivision of work is based on quite different grounds than specialization. Where specialization leads to more intensive development of skill and ability, subdivision leads to a limitation of skills and ability.[4]

The mass-production line is the classic illustration of the subdivision of work. Historically it is contrasted with the specialization of the skilled worker in the shop. The association, then, observed between an organic management style and unit firms, and a mechanical style and mass-production operations is consistent with the hypothesized relationship between management style and work subdivision or specialization.

In process firms the relation between subdivision and specialization of work is still under consideration by organizational analysts, but there appears to be a general trend toward greater specialization and away from subdivision.[5]

The style of management, however, is most directly related to the occupational tasks of supervisory personnel in the firm, and it is hypothesized that employment differences among supervisors parallel those observed among production workers. Specifically, it is hypothesized that unit and process firms concentrate a greater proportion of their supervisory force in nonroutinized administrative positions than is the case for large-batch and mass-production firms, the latter having a considerably larger portion of their supervisory force at the level of direct production supervision. It was expected, then, that unit and process firms would have the lowest ratio of supervisors to managers, and large-batch and mass-production firms the highest ratio.

The data on the 55 Minneapolis firms confirmed the expected relationship. It was observed that the median ratio of supervisors to managers for large-batch and mass-production firms was 4 to 1, while it was only 2 to 1 in the case of unit and process firms. The differences observed between the mass-production firms and the others increased when only the very successful firms were compared with one another, the median ratio of supervisors to managers of the very successful large-batch and mass-production firms being 8 to 1 compared with only 2 to 1 for the very successful unit and process firms (Table 16).

TABLE 16

PRODUCTION TECHNOLOGY, RATIO OF SUPERVISORS TO MANAGERS, AND LEVEL OF BUSINESS SUCCESS IN MINNEAPOLIS FIRMS

RATIO OF SUPERVISORS TO MANAGERS AND LEVEL OF SUCCESS	TECHNOLOGY					
	Unit and Small-Batch		Mass		Process	
	No.	%	No.	%	No.	%
All Firms						
1 or less	8	44	7	25	—	—
2–3	6	33	6	21	3	60
4–5	4	22	6	21	2	40
6–10	—	—	3	11	—	—
11 or more	—	—	6	21	—	—
Total	18	99	28	99	5	100
Median	2		4		2	
No information	1		2		1	
Very Successful Firms						
1 or less	3	33	3	23	—	—
2–3	4	44	2	15	3	60
4–5	2	22	1	8	2	40
6–10	—	—	2	15	—	—
11 or more	—	—	5	38	—	—
Total	9	99	13	99	5	100
Median	2		8		2	
No information	1		2		1	

The implications of these data for the Marxian analysis are simple and direct. The change in style of management associated with changing production technologies is accompanied by parallel changes in the labor force and the nature of work in the industrial complex. It appears that the relations of production moved from a relatively high degree of specialization, at both the worker and supervisory level, in unit-production technologies to a relatively high degree of subdivision of work at both levels in large-batch and mass-production industries. The trend for the future under continuous process or automated technologies seems to reverse this process, inclining toward the specialization characteristic of earlier forms of manufacturing operations.

Promotion Policy

Related to the above considerations is the question of the organizations policy with respect to advancement of personnel within the organization. Some firms make a practice of advancing from within, while others are very likely to hire from the outside to fill administrative vacancies. Woodward reports a direct relationship between advancement policy and technological complexity.

With respect to promotion in Essex industry, Woodward reported that 30 percent of the firms studied promoted only from within the organization, while 70 percent recruited some of their managers from the outside.[6] She saw the problem of internal or external recruitment in terms of the presence or absence of a managerial culture, as appears in her comment on the managers of process industries:

In general the behaviour of managers was conditioned more by their position in the organization than by their personalities. An extreme example of this was found in one large continuous-flow plant, where there had been 100 per cent turnover of managerial and supervisory staff above the rank of foreman in three and a half years. Some of the staff had been promoted from one job to another, but many had come in during that period from the company's other production units, from universities, or from outside firms. In spite of this the factory operated very successfully and it seemed that, in all vital respects, one plant manager behaved in very much the same way as his predecessor had done or as his successor was likely to do.[7]

Although no data are presented, the gist of Woodward's argument is that promotion from within an organization is most important in unit and small-batch operations where nontechnical decision making reflects the needs of a unique industry. On the other hand, an internal type of promotional system is least important in process firms where decisions are highly technical and where supervisory and managerial personnel are most interchangeable because of the sharing of a general technological orientation.[8] The relation between the advancement policy, production technology, and operating success has a bearing on the general desirability of promotion from within.[9] From the Essex study it can be inferred that a policy of promoting exclusively from within[10] would most often be found in unit and small-batch operations and least often in process industries, mass-production operations falling between the other two.

The Minneapolis data strongly support this inference

(Table 17): 79 percent of the unit firms, 67 percent of the mass-production firms and only 18 percent of the process firms had policies of promoting only from within the organization. The relationship observed is stronger when only the very successful firms are compared with one another. One hundred percent of the very successful unit production firms, 73 percent of the mass-production, and 18 percent of the process firms promote from within.

TABLE 17

PRODUCTION TECHNOLOGY, LEVEL OF BUSINESS SUCCESS, AND PROMOTION POLICY IN MINNEAPOLIS FIRMS

TECHNOLOGY AND LEVEL OF SUCCESS	PROMOTION POLICY					
	Promote from Within		Mixed Promotion Policy		Total	
	No.	%	No.	%	No.	%
All Firms						
Unit	15	79	4	21	19	100
Mass	20	67	10	33	30	100
Process	1	17	5	83	6	100
Very Successful Firms						
Unit	10	100	—	—	10	100
Mass	11	73	4	27	15	100
Process	1	17	5	83	6	100

The hypothesized link between technology and advancement policy within a firm is supported by the replication data. Furthermore, the relationship is more distinct when only the very successful firms were compared with one another. However, a considerable difference was found between the English and Minneapolis samples with respect to the proportion of firms having a policy of promoting exclusively from within: 30 percent of the Essex firms compared with 65 percent of the Minneapolis firms.

Labor Costs

The relation between labor costs and production technology was also examined. In the Essex sample the percentage of costs allocated to wages was considerably less for process firms than for the other two types. The median cost allocation was 15 percent for process as opposed to 30–35 percent for the unit and mass-production firms.[11] The direction of the relationship was similar though somewhat weaker for the Minneapolis sample (Table 18). Furthermore, the relationship was attenuated when only the very successful firms were compared. The median percentages of cost allocation of the total were 25 for process, 36 for unit, and 35 for mass-production firms. For very successful firms the medians were 25 percent for the process, 33 percent for the unit, and 32 percent for the mass-production firms. Another difference observed between the three types of production systems was the proportion of firms having labor costs of 50 percent or greater—43 percent of the unit operations, 26 percent of the mass production, and 20 percent of the process firms. The differences observed for the sample as a whole corresponded to those observed for very successful firms.

The relationships between labor characteristics and production technology reported by Woodward were replicated in the Minneapolis sample.

TABLE 18

PRODUCTION TECHNOLOGY, LEVEL OF BUSINESS SUCCESS, AND LABOR COSTS IN MINNEAPOLIS AND ESSEX FIRMS

TECHNOLOGY AND LEVEL OF SUCCESS	LABOR COSTS								Total	
	Under 12½%		12½–25%		26–50%		Over 50%			
	No.	%	No.	%	No.	%	No.	%	No.	%
All Minneapolis Firms										
Unit: Range	2	14	1	7	5	36	6	43	14	100
Median					36					
Mass: Range	2	11	1	5	11	58	5	26	19	100
Median					35					
Process: Range			3	60	1	20	1	20	5	100
Median			25							
All Essex Firms										
Unit: Range	1	4	4	17	14	61	4	17	23	99
Median					36					
Mass: Range	1	4	10	36	11	39	6	21	28	100
Median					34					
Process: Range	8	40	12	60					20	100
Median			15							
Very Successful Minneapolis Firms										
Unit: Range	1	11	1	11	3	33	4	44	9	99
Median					33					
Mass: Range			1	10	7	70	2	20	10	100
Median					32					
Process: Range			3	60	1	20	1	20	5	20
Median			25							

SIZE AND LABOR

As in the case of the organizational characteristics already considered, arguments could be (and in some cases have been) made that the number of personnel is a determinant of labor characteristics.

Ratio of Production to Nonproduction Workers

Caplow argued an ecological correlation between ratio of production to nonproduction workers and the general size of the industrial organizational units at different time periods.[12] The ratio has, he insisted, declined through time in the United States simultaneously with a general increase in size of industrial organizations. He argued that the size of the labor force is a determinant of the ratio of production to nonproduction workers. The Essex study failed to bear this out. Nor did the Minneapolis data support the hypothesized relationship between size of labor force and ratio of production to nonproduction workers (Appendix 4, Table 43). The ranges of values of the ratios were similar for the larger and the smaller firms—those with more than 1,000 workers and those with 1,000 or fewer employees. The median values for the ratios were close. In the case of the total sample the median ratios were 3 for the smaller firms and 2 for the larger firms, while for only the very successful firms the median ratios were the same—2 for the smaller and 2 for the larger.

Ratio of Supervisors to Managers

The ratio of supervisors to managers differed slightly between the larger and smaller firms, the larger firms having somewhat higher ratios. The differences were slight, however, and were a direct function of the correlation between size of labor force and technology. The median ratio for the larger firms was 4, compared with 2 for the smaller firms (Appendix 4, Table 44). The differences between the medians was exclusively a function of the fact that all of the higher ratios were associated with mass-production operations which tend to be larger than the others. No differences between mass-production firms of differing size are observed with respect to the ratio of supervisors to managers.

The apparent relation between size and ratio of supervisors to managers vanished when the interaction of technology and size was investigated.

Promotion Policy

No relation between advancement policy and size of the labor force was found. About two-thirds of the smaller and two-thirds of the larger firms had policies of advancing from within (Appendix 4, Table 45).

Labor Costs

The relation between size and labor costs were as strong as that observed in the case of production technology. In neither was it impressive: the median wage costs for the larger firms was 28 percent compared with 38 percent for the smaller firms. For the very successful firms the median values were 28 percent in the larger ones and 35 percent in the smaller firms.

The original relationship observed between technology and labor costs was weak, and the confounding of this relationship with another one of the same magnitude makes it unlikely that the meaning of these can be interpreted in the context of this empirical analysis.

Size of labor force was not independently related to any of the labor characteristics under examination. The single possible exception was labor costs—an indeterminate relationship at this point.

Insofar as Woodward's analysis is under test here it survives very nicely. The relative effect of size is negligible, and none of the relationships between technology and labor were challenged by the findings of the replication.

Technology and the Separation of Ownership and Management

The effect of the separation of ownership and management on labor characteristics may be quite significant. It could be hypothesized that this separation is related to each of the labor characteristics under consideration.

It is not unreasonable to assume that owner-managers strive for control of the organization by concentrating personnel at the lowest levels of the organization, thus increasing the ratio of production to nonproduction workers.

It is conceivable that the ratio of supervisors to managers might be quite high in firms with combined ownership and management as the owner-management strives to maintain distance and reduce the threat of control being wrested from him. Promotion policy in firms with combined ownership and management could be predicted to focus on advancement from within because of the highly personal nature of the operation. Finally, the generally smaller capitalization of firms with combined ownership and management could be expected to result in a more labor-intensive operation with proportionately higher labor costs than for firms with separated ownership and management.

RATIO OF PRODUCTION TO NONPRODUCTION WORKERS

The anticipated relationship between the separation of ownership and management and the ratio of production workers was observed for the sample as a whole: the median ratio was 3.5 for firms with combined ownership and management, compared with 2 firms where these are separated (Table 19).

The data on the relationship between separation of ownership and management and the ratio of production to nonproduction workers (Table 19) fulfill expectations. The median ratio of production to nonproduction workers for firms with owner-managers was 3.5, compared with 2 for firms which separated ownership and management. The anticipated relationship persisted when only the very successful

TABLE 19

SEPARATION OF OWNERSHIP AND MANAGEMENT, RATIO OF PRODUCTION TO NONPRODUCTION WORKERS, AND LEVEL OF BUSINESS SUCCESS IN MINNEAPOLIS FIRMS

RATIO OF PRODUCTION TO NONPRODUCTION WORKERS AND LEVEL OF SUCCESS	OWNERSHIP AND MANAGEMENT			
	Combined		Separated	
	No.	%	No.	%
All Firms				
1 or less	2	12	12	31
2–3	6	38	17	44
4–5	3	19	7	18
6 or more	5	31	3	7
Total	16	100	39	100
Median	3.5		2	
Very Successful Firms				
1 or less	1	17	10	40
2–3	3	50	9	36
4–5	2	33	3	12
6 or more	—	—	3	12
Total	6	100	25	100
Median	3		2	

were compared with one another, although it was not strengthened.

This finding raises the question as to the interactive effects of production technology and the separation of ownership and management on production-nonproduction worker ratios. Unfortunately for the analysis of this possibility among very successful firms with combined ownership and management, there was only one mass-production firm and one process firm—far too few to permit generalization. Furthermore, among very successful unit firms with separated ownership and management the majority were unit operations engaged in the manufacture of very complex products—a factor demonstrated to be related to the ratio of production workers in unit-production firms. Hence the data are inadequate for a serious testing of the potential influence of the effect of separation of ownership and management upon the ratio of production to nonproduction workers.

What can be said is that the ratio of production workers was rather high among unit operation firms with combined ownership and management, the median being 4. The ratio of production to nonproduction workers among mass-production firms with separated management and ownership was somewhat less than that for the unit firms with combined ownership and management—2 compared with 4. Among process firms with separated ownership and management the ratio of production to nonproduction workers was quite low, the median value being 0.70.

The ranges and median values of the ratio of production to nonproduction workers for the unit firms with combined ownership and management, and for the mass-production and process firms with separated ownership and management, are consistent with the argument that production technology is a significant determinant of the ratio of production to nonproduction workers. Unfortunately, the data from the Minneapolis study are inadequate to elaborate this complex relationship further.

RATIO OF SUPERVISORS TO MANAGERS

It was hypothesized that firms with owner-managers would have a higher ratio of supervisors to managers than firms with separated ownership and management. The reverse was found (Table 20).

The median ratio of supervisors to managers for all firms with combined ownership and management was 2, and 3 for firms with separated ownership and management. When very successful firms were compared, the median number of supervisors to managers for those with combined ownership and management was only 1, compared with 4 for those with separated ownership and management.

This finding was consistent with the fact that a greater proportion of unit-operation firms had combined ownership and management, while the greater proportion of mass-production firms had separated ownership and management.

The observed lack of a meaningful relationship between the separation of ownership and management and the ratio of supervisors to managers was reinforced when the data relating to the relative importance of production technology and the separation of ownership and management as determinants of the ratio of supervisors to managers were examined. The successful unit operations with combined ownership and management had a median ratio of one supervisor per manager compared with nine for the successful

TABLE 20

RATIO OF SUPERVISORS TO MANAGERS BY OWNERSHIP TYPE AND LEVEL OF BUSINESS SUCCESS IN MINNEAPOLIS FIRMS

RATIO OF SUPERVISORS TO MANAGERS	OWNERSHIP AND MANAGEMENT							
	COMBINED				SEPARATED			
	Level of Success				Level of Success			
	Successful		All Firms		Successful		All Firms	
	No.	%	No.	%	No.	%	No.	%
Less than 1	3	50	6	38	2	10	6	17
1			1	6	1	5	2	6
2	2	33	5	31	5	23	8	23
3					2	10	2	6
4			3	19	4	19	7	20
5	1	17	1	6			1	3
6								
7							1	3
8					1	5	1	3
9								
10					1	5	1	3
11 or more					5	23	6	17
Total	6	100	16	100	21	100	35	102
Median	1		2		4		3	

TABLE 21
SEPARATION OF OWNERSHIP AND MANAGEMENT, PROMOTION POLICY, AND LEVEL OF BUSINESS SUCCESS IN MINNEAPOLIS FIRMS

ADVANCEMENT POLICY	OWNERSHIP AND MANAGEMENT							
	COMBINED				SEPARATED			
	Level of Success				Level of Success			
	Successful		All Firms		Successful		All Firms	
	No.	%	No.	%	No.	%	No.	%
Promote from within the organization	5	83	11	69	17	68	25	64
Mixed: some advancement from within and some hiring from the outside	1	17	5	31	8	32	14	36
Total	6	100	16	100	25	100	39	100

mass-production operations with separated ownership and management and two for the process firms with separated ownership and management—technology being obviously correlated with the ratio of supervisors to managers while the separation of ownership and management was not.

Promotion Policy

It was hypothesized that firms with combined ownership and management would be more likely to promote from within than firms with separated ownership and management. The Minneapolis data did not confirm the hypothesis (Table 21).

However, successful firms with combined ownership and management more frequently had a policy of advancing from within. Five of these successful firms with such policies were unit operations; the single successful mass-production firm with combined ownership and management had a policy of mixed advancement.

There was no evidence that the separation of ownership and management had any effect upon the promotion policy of the industrial firms of Minneapolis sample.

Labor Costs

A possibility of a relation between the separation of ownership and management and labor costs was anticipated. It was suggested that labor costs would be higher for firms with combined ownership and management and lower for firms with separated ownership and management. The data on these variables confirm the hypothesis (Table 22). The median percentage labor costs for firms with combined ownership and management was 50 percent, both for the success-

TABLE 22

SEPARATION OF OWNERSHIP AND MANAGEMENT, LABOR COSTS, AND LEVEL OF BUSINESS SUCCESS IN MINNEAPOLIS FIRMS

PERCENTAGE OF LABOR COSTS	OWNERSHIP AND MANAGEMENT							
	COMBINED				SEPARATED			
	Level of Success				Level of Success			
	Successful		All Firms		Successful		All Firms	
	No.	%	No.	%	No.	%	No.	%
0–12½%					1	5	4	14
22½–25%	2	40	2	22	5	26	5	17
26–50%			1	11	9	48	14	48
Greater than 50%	3	60	6	67	4	21	6	21
Total	5	100	9	100	19	100	29	100
Median	50%		50%		30%		30%	

ful firms and for the total sample, while the median percentage labor costs for firms with separated ownership and management was 30 percent, both for the total sample and for the very successful firms.

The relationship may hold even when the effects of production technology are taken into account.

Of mass-production firms with combined ownership and management, only two reported their labor costs. For the unit-operation firms with combined ownership and management, the median percentage of labor costs for all firms was reported at 50 percent, and for the very successful firms at 55 percent.

No variation in labor costs were observed for firms with separated ownership and management when the various production technologies were compared. The median percentage of labor cost for process firms was 27 percent, compared with 30 percent for mass-production firms and 32 percent for the unit-operation firms with separated ownership and management.

As Woodward notes, a number of factors affect labor costs, but in the analysis of the Minneapolis firms there was not much basis for considering production technology to be one of them.

The analysis of the relation between the separation of ownership and management and labor characteristics of the Minneapolis firms revealed a strong tie with labor costs, but little else. No relation was observed between the ratio of supervisors to managers and the promotion policies of the firms. The relationship between the separation of ownership and management and the ratio of production to nonproduction workers seems to be produced primarily by two technological variables: type of production technology, as reported by Woodward, and the technical complexity of the product —a factor increasing the proportion of technical, professional, and other forms of nonproduction labor.

SUMMARY

The analysis of the relation between production technology and labor characteristics of Minneapolis firms supported the findings of the Essex study. Size of labor force was observed to bear virtually no relationship to the labor variables. The separation of ownership and management was related only to labor costs.

The analysis of production technology and labor supported Woodward's analysis. Hence it also supports her implied assumption that organizational theory must tear the relevant variables out of their historical and ideological Marxian and classical economic contexts, recombining them into an empirically more useful model for the adequate understanding of industrial organization and operation.

Having considered to some extent a reevaluation of the variables central to Marxian theory—the means and the relations of production—it is only logical to turn to reconsider and reevaluate some of the variables worked up in classical economic interpretation. A most reasonable social variable critical to the classical scheme was the marketplace. Since it mediates the industrial firm and the wider society and, vice versa, it is plausible to look beyond it in the light of the wider social milieu.

NOTES

1. Joan Woodward, *Industrial Organization: Theory and Practice* (London: Oxford University Press, 1965), p. 59.

2. See Chapter 3.

3. Robert Dubin, *The World of Work: Industrial Society and Human Relations* (Englewood Cliffs, N.J.: Prentice-Hall, 1958), esp. Chap. 10.

4. Ibid., p. 179.

5. Ibid., Chap. 11, and Ewan Clague and Leon Greenberg, "Employment," in *Automation, and Technological Change,* ed. John T. Dunlop (Englewood Cliffs, N.J.: Prentice-Hall, 1962), pp. 114–131.

6. Woodward, *Industrial Organization,* p. 30.

7. Joan Woodward, *Management and Technology* (London: Department of Scientific and Industrial Research, Her Majesty's Stationery Office, 1958).

8. The implications of these observations for the controversy over the consequences of managerial succession are direct and quite important. See, for example, Alvin Gouldner, *Patterns of Industrial Bureaucracy* (New York: The Free Press, 1954), and Robert H. Guest, *Organizational Change: The Effect of Successful Leadership* (Homewood, Ill.: Richard D. Irwin, 1962).

9. The writings of James Worthy provide an example of the

kinds of arguments presented in favor of a policy of promoting from within. See James C. Worthy, *Big Business and Free Men* (New York: Harper & Row, Publishers, 1959), and "Factors Influencing Employee Morale," *Harvard Business Review* 28 (January, 1950):61–73.

10. It is assumed that very few companies are in a position actually to restrict advancement to existing personnel, but that the company policy is significant here as an indication of the relative importance placed upon this labor-related variable.

11. Woodward, *Industrial Organization,* p. 54.

12. Theodore Caplow, "Organizational Size," *Administrative Science Quarterly* 1 (March, 1957):484–505.

6

THE SOCIAL MILIEU

In the course of replicating Woodward's study of industry and technology in southeast Essex it has been necessary to reevaluate one of the critical concerns of Marxian analysis, namely the linkages between the modes and the relations of production. Woodward's findings and the replication confirm the hypothesis that the modes of production are one determinant of the organizational characteristics of industry. Both the Marxian and the classical positions are changed when the Marxian variables are torn from their original ideological context and combined into a new explanation of industrial organization and function. Hence there is no logical reason for terminating analysis at the point where only the variables central to the Marxian position have been reconsidered.

Since reconsideration of industrial organization in terms of variables central to Marxism has yielded interesting results, it would seem quite appropriate also to consider variables central to the classical perspective. This, indeed, would carry our analysis to a stage beyond the original plan of replicating Woodward's study.

The marketplace played an important role in the classical position. Economic production was the key to all else that occurred in society, inasmuch as it supplied the basic utilities that made it possible. However, the marketplace mediated the industrial enterprise and the wider society: through it society was supplied with economic utilities; from it the industrial enterprise obtained various categories of things it required for its operations, including labor.

The one thing the classical thinkers assumed could always be counted on was the pursuit by the individual of his self-interest. Manifest under properly policed supervision, the pitting of self-interest against self-interest could only result in the maximum utility of all. Market competition would inevitably favor the achievement of the most efficient industrial form. These in turn would achieve the highest level of success in the marketplace. When Woodward first began her study by attempting to correlate the various properties of industrial organizations with economic success she was, as noted earlier, working solidly within this tradition.

Even the pioneers of the classical tradition, however,

were well aware of the fact that the conception of the marketplace as an institution maximizing rational efficiency because of the self-interest of a plurality of buyers and sellers operating under rules of fair competition was often more an ideal than a reality. Governments often exceeded their proper role of exercising the minimum police power to keep competition fair, and in various ways interfered with the operations of the marketplace. Businessmen often colluded to fix prices or sought to monopolize markets. Sellers, including the sellers of labor, united to bargain collectively, securing more advantageous terms than they could as individuals. All such factors prevented realization of the ideal situation of a plurality of buyers and sellers each promoting his self-interest in the most rationally efficient manner possible.

Furthermore, as nineteenth-century western society assumed more and more the characteristic features of contemporary capitalism, it became evident that the notion of individuals operating on the basis of rational self-interest was more ideological than empirical. Individuals and pluralities of individuals often behaved traditionalistically, affectively, or evaluatively[1] rather than rationally. In fact if not in theory, businessmen often found it expedient to expand their operations far outside the market proper. They began to advertise and to "educate" the public at large. In short, they attempted to manipulate the wider social milieu to create an atmosphere favorable to their operations.

Taking all these things into account, it becomes painfully evident that even if one focuses on industrial organization and success, the problem is complicated. A business can be "successful" for many reasons: because it secures favorable legislation from various relevant political structures, because of the skill of its public relations specialists, because of the efficacy of its advertising campaigns, because of the shrewdness of its policies in establishing liaisons with other industries, because of its skill in handling labor problems and—last but not least—because of its sheer efficiency in rationally meeting the demands of its customers more effectively than its rivals.

All these considerations were important in the present study in the decision to go beyond a mere replication of Woodward to a consideration of some of the influences on industrial organization and success of a variety of market and general milieu variables. This study will seek not to exhaust the possibilities, but merely to make a beginning of their examinations.

MARKET AND MILIEU VARIABLES

An analysis of milieu variables beginning with a consideration of the marketplace is important because of its centrality to the classical tradition, and because it represents a point of convergence in the liberal and radical traditions. It is also important because changes in milieu variables (e.g., the shift from a competitive to an administered market, the shift from combined ownership and management of small industrial units to the separation of ownership and management in the context of giant corporations, and the emergence of affluent economies) are often cited[2] as the primary reasons for failures in the predictions of both classical and radical interpretations of the industrial complex and industrial organizations.

One market variable was investigated empirically in the Minneapolis replications and will initiate consideration of the social milieu in this chapter. Following a discussion of this variable an attempt will be made to interpret the differences observed between the English and Minneapolis studies as primarily a function of differences in the socioeconomic milieus containing these two sets of industries.

Dependence on the Local Market

A manufacturing industry may become dependent upon a given market in a variety of ways, two of the more important being dependence for material inputs and dependence for outputs-sales. The Minneapolis study included questions regarding the extent to which the industries were dependent upon local markets, the Twin Cities area, for production supplies and for sales.

These questions were included because it was anticipated that the relationships here would be a direct function of technological complexity. It was reasoned that the uncertainties associated with unit and small-batch production would force close ties with local markets for the acquisition of production supplies, the unpredictable production schedules making the scheduling of raw materials difficult and forcing the establishment of linkages to convenient source.

On the other hand, the predictability of production schedules of process operations should make local suppliers less important, freeing the organization for purchasing on the basis of competitive pricing, and this should result in less reliance on local markets. It was theorized that mass-production firms would fall between unit and process operations in this respect and it was predicted that they would be more dependent than process firms, but less dependent than unit and small-batch operations on local suppliers.

The data bearing on this relationship are presented in Table 23. The predicted relationship is observed in this case, 68 percent of the unit operations being rather dependent upon local markets for production supplies, com-

TABLE 23

PRODUCTION TECHNOLOGY AND ORGANIZATIONAL DEPENDENCE ON LOCAL MARKETS FOR PRODUCTION MATERIALS IN MINNEAPOLIS FIRMS

LEVEL OF SUCCESS AND DEPENDENCE ON LOCAL MARKETS FOR PRODUCTION SUPPLIES	TECHNOLOGY					
	Unit and Small-Batch		Large-Batch and Mass		Process	
	No.	%	No.	%	No.	%
All Firms						
Considerably dependent	13	68	14	47	1	17
Little or no dependence	6	32	16	53	5	83
Total	19	100	30	100	6	100
Very Successful Firms						
Considerably dependent	17	70	8	53	1	17
Little or no dependence	3	30	7	47	5	83
Total	10	100	15	100	6	100

pared with only 47 percent of the mass-production operations and 17 percent of the process firms. This relationship is not strengthened appreciably when only the successful firms are examined.

As was the case with the other organizational variables being considered, it is possible that the relationship observed here could be a function of the relationship between local market dependence and the other independent variables studied—separation of ownership and management, and size of firm.

In the case of the separation of ownership and management the data are unambiguous. Half of the firms with combined ownership and management were primarily dependent on local markets for production supplies, while 51 percent of the firms with separated ownership and management were also considerably dependent (Appendix 5, Table 48).

A possible relationship emerged when only the very successful firms were compared with one another, but this was strictly a function of the relationship between technology and the separation of ownership and management. Eighty-three percent (5/6) of the very successful firms with combined ownership and management were observed to be dependent upon local markets for supplies, compared with only 44 percent (11/25) of those with separated ownership and management. In this case the five successful firms with combined ownership and management which were dependent on local markets were unit operations and the sixth, which was not dependent, was a mass-production operation. Among the successful firms with separated ownership and management, only four of the twenty-five firms are unit and small-batch operations while the remaining firms are large-batch, mass-production, or process operations.

The relationship between size of the firm and dependence on local markets for production supplies is somewhat more complex than that observed in the case of the separation of ownership and management. The smaller firms were more likely to be dependent upon local markets than the larger ones—57 percent of those with labor forces of 1,000 or less compared with 40 percent of those with labor forces in excess of 1,000 being considerably dependent upon the local markets for production materials (Table 24).

TABLE 24

SIZE OF LABOR FORCE AND DEPENDENCE UPON LOCAL MARKETS FOR PRODUCTION MATERIALS IN MINNEAPOLIS FIRMS

LEVEL OF SUCCESS AND DEPENDENCE ON LOCAL MARKETS FOR PRODUCTION SUPPLIES	SIZE OF LABOR FORCE			
	1,000 or less		More Than 1,000	
	No.	%	No.	%
All Firms				
Considerably dependent	20	57	8	40
Little or no dependence	15	43	12	60
Total	35	100	20	100
Very Successful Firms				
Considerably dependent	10	62	6	40
Little or no dependence	6	38	9	60
Total	16	100	15	100

No strengthening of the relationship was observed when only the very successful firms were compared with one another, but further examination of the data revealed the possibility of a complex relationship between production technology, size of labor force, and dependence upon local markets for supplies. Among the unit operations it appeared that the larger firms were more dependent upon local markets for supplies—80 percent of those over 1,000 (4/5) compared with 63 percent (9/14) of those smaller[3]—while in the case of mass-production and process operations the larger firms showed somewhat less dependence upon the local markets than their smaller counterparts—33 to 56 percent in the case of mass-production firms and 0 to 33 percent in the case of process firms (Table 25).

In any event, the relationship between technology and dependence on local markets for supplies was maintained even when size was the control; 64 percent of the small unit operations were considerably dependent compared with 56 percent of the smaller mass-production operations and 33 percent of the process firms. For the larger firms, 80 percent of the unit operations, 33 percent of the mass-production firms, and none of the process firms were considerably dependent upon the local markets in this respect.

The hypothesized relationship between technology and economic dependence on local markets is supported by these data, although the relationship between size and this form of dependence is not clear from the data.

With respect to dependence on local markets for sales, the relationship hypothesized here was exactly the reverse of that for dependence on production supplied. Precisely the same set of factors—unpredictable production schedules

TABLE 25

PRODUCTION TECHNOLOGY, SIZE OF LABOR FORCE, AND DEPENDENCE UPON LOCAL MARKETS FOR PRODUCTION MATERIALS IN MINNEAPOLIS FIRMS

TECHNOLOGY AND DEPENDENCE ON LOCAL MARKETS FOR PRODUCTION SUPPLIES	SIZE OF LABOR FORCE			
	1,000 or less		More Than 1,000	
	No.	%	No.	%
Unit and Small-Batch				
Considerably dependent	9	64	4	80
Little or no dependence	5	36	1	20
Total	14	100	5	100
Large-Batch and Mass				
Considerably dependent	10	56	4	33
Little or no dependence	8	44	8	67
Total	18	100	12	100
Process				
Considerably dependent	1	33	—	—
Little or no dependence	2	67	3	100
Total	3	100	3	100

—that would lead a unit operation into a relationship of dependence on the local economy could lead it to expand its market. The easiest way for a unit operation to control uncertainty in production would be to seek orders from the widest market possible, the effect of this being to iron out the irregularities of economic activity always present in a limited market and to avoid the repercussions of local periods of economic boom and recession.

The process firms, however, are confronted with another sort of problem in the area of sales. The capital investment in process-manufacturing equipment is considerable and return on the investment requires, very often, successful operation over a long period of time. All of this implies the desirability of market control, the best way to make accurate market projections. It may be anticipated then that process firms would attempt to gain a guaranteed share of local markets, the assumption being that local markets are easier to control and to predict than are larger economic networks. Hence the hypothesis that unit and small-batch firms would be the least dependent on local markets for sales, while process firms would be the most dependent on local markets for sales, mass-production operations falling somewhere between the other two.

The data on the relationship between production technology and dependence on local markets for sales are presented in Table 26. The predicted relationship is only partially observed. Unit and small-batch operations were found less likely to manifest dependence on local markets for sales than mass-production firms, 32 percent of the unit operations compared with 47 percent of the mass-production firms. However, unit operations were no less dependent on local markets than process firms, 32 percent of the unit compared with 33 percent of process firms being dependent in this respect. The relationship was not appreciably strengthened when only the very successful firms were compared.

As was the case with dependence on local markets for production materials, no relationship was observed between separation of ownership and management and dependence on local markets for sales, 38 percent of the firms with combined ownership and management being considerably dependent compared with 41 percent of the firms with separated ownership and management (Appendix 5, Table 49).

TABLE 26

PRODUCTION TECHNOLOGY, LEVEL OF BUSINESS SUCCESS, AND ORGANIZATIONAL DEPENDENCE ON LOCAL MARKETS FOR SALES IN MINNEAPOLIS FIRMS

LEVEL OF SUCCESS AND DEPENDENCE ON LOCAL MARKETS FOR SALES	TECHNOLOGY					
	Unit and Small-Batch		Large-Batch and Mass		Process	
	No.	%	No.	%	No.	%
All Firms						
Considerably dependent	6	32	14	47	2	33
Little or no dependence	13	68	16	53	4	67
Total	19	100	30	100	6	100
Very Successful Firms						
Considerably dependent	3	30	8	53	2	33
Little or no dependence	7	70	7	47	4	67
Total	10	100	15	100	6	100

The relationship observed between size of the labor force and dependence on local markets for sales was of the same form as that observed for relationship between size of labor force and dependence on local markets for production materials, the larger firms being less likely to be dependent than smaller ones (Table 27). In this case the relationship appeared to be quite strong, 51 percent of the smaller firms reporting considerable dependence on local markets for sales, compared with only 20 percent of the larger firms. Furthermore, this relationship was strengthened somewhat when only the very successful firms were compared with one another, 62 percent of the successful smaller firms reporting dependence compared with only 20 percent of the larger firms.

TABLE 27

SIZE OF LABOR FORCE, LEVEL OF BUSINESS SUCCESS, AND ORGANIZATIONAL DEPENDENCE ON LOCAL MARKETS FOR SALES IN MINNEAPOLIS FIRMS

LEVEL OF SUCCESS AND DEPENDENCE ON LOCAL MARKETS FOR SALES	SIZE OF LABOR FORCE			
	1,000 or less		More Than 1,000	
	No.	%	No.	%
All Firms				
Considerably dependent	18	51	4	20
Little or no dependence	17	49	16	80
Total	35	100	20	100
Very Successful Firms				
Considerably dependent	10	62	3	20
Little or no dependence	6	38	12	80
Total	16	100	15	100

When we examined the complex relationship between production technology, size of labor force, and dependence upon local markets for sales, the data were suggestive regarding the relative effect of the two independent variables. It appears (Table 28) that the predicted relationship between production technology and dependence on local mar-

TABLE 28
PRODUCTION TECHNOLOGY, SIZE OF LABOR FORCE, AND ORGANIZATIONAL DEPENDENCE ON LOCAL MARKETS FOR SALES IN MINNEAPOLIS FIRMS

TECHNOLOGY AND DEPENDENCE ON LOCAL MARKETS FOR SALES	SIZE OF LABOR FORCE			
	1,000 or less		More Than 1,000	
	No.	%	No.	%
Unit and Small-Batch				
Considerably dependent	6	43	—	—
Little or no dependence	8	57	5	100
Total	14	100	5	100
Large-Batch and Mass				
Considerably dependent	10	56	4	33
Little or no dependence	8	44	8	67
Total	18	100	12	100
Process				
Considerably dependent	2	67	—	—
Little or no dependence	1	33	3	100
Total	3	100	3	100

kets for sales was characteristic of only the smaller firms, all but four (4/20) of the larger firms not being dependent on local markets in this fashion. For the smaller firms, 43 percent of the unit and small-batch, 56 percent of the mass-production, and 67 percent of the process firms reported considerable dependence on local markets for sales. None of the larger small-batch or process firms and only 33 percent of the mass-production firms reported such a dependence. The predicted relationship, then, obtained for the smaller firms but not the larger.

The data bearing on organizational dependence on local markets, both for the acquisition of production materials and for sales, generally supported the hypothesized relationship between production technology and economic ties to the local economic community. Size of firm, as indicated by size of labor force, appeared to influence this relationship, particularly in regard to dependence on local markets for sales, the relationship having appeared only for the smaller firms and not for the larger ones when sales dependency was considered.

The relationship between size of the firm and local economic dependence is not surprising, nor does it bring into question the basic relationship of concern in this analysis —that between type of production technology and industrial organization. Growth in the scale of an industrial organization has often been a step taken to strengthen the economic position of organizations with respect to the accumulation of capital to hedge against lean times and to the increase in market area to avoid vicissitudes of local conditions. It appears from the data analyzed here that dependency on local economic arenas is a function of both size and technology.

The implications of these findings for the study of the relationships between industrial organizations and other economic organizations and between industrial organization and the community are direct and interesting. It can be hypothesized that local economic dependencies strongly influence the entrance of an economic organization into community affairs, those directly related to its operation as mediated by associations made up of economic elites and those indirectly related to its operation as mediated by general civic associations and activities.

These data would suggest the possibility that smaller industrial organizations, which by virtue of their production technology are economically dependent on the community, are forced into participation in the social networks of the community, whereas the larger organizations, which have freed themselves from dependence on the local economic community, map exercise an option with respect to participation in the life of the community. More generally stated, the participation of economically dependent industrial organizations in the life of the community is explicable in terms of the economic position of these organizations, while the participation of less dependent industrial organizatons represents the exercise of an option on the part of the industrial elite. The economic necessity driving the dependent units may account for part of the purported narrowness and conservatism of small-scale economic leaders in the affairs of the community, while the somewhat wider scope of participation often attributed to elites in large-scale economic units may partially result from the fact that their activity is optional and therefore more likely to occur when individuals act with respect to what they consider to be more basic social conditions.

The data gathered and analyzed in the Minneapolis study are, in any event, sufficiently suggestive to warrant further study on the linkage between technology, economic position in the local community, and participation in community affairs.

NOTES

1. These types of actions follow Max Weber; see Max Weber, *The Theory of Social and Economic Organization,* trans. A. M. Henderson and Talcott Parsons (New York: Oxford University Press, 1947), pp. 87ff.

2. A very persuasive case for this position is presented in John K. Galbraith, *The New Industrial State* (Boston: Houghton Mifflin Company, 1967).

3. This finding is not consistent with the often proposed simple and direct relationship between economic scale and social independence of local areas.

7

THE CONFRONTATION OF MARXIAN AND CLASSICAL THEORIES OF ORGANIZATION

The general conclusion of this analysis, consistent with Woodward's, is that there are direct links between production technology and the organizational characteristics of the firms studied. Further, the kinds of linkages observed in the Minneapolis setting are quite similar to those observed in the southeast Essex area.[1]

In reflecting on the Minneapolis survey, several kinds of comments, by way of summary, are in order. These considerations will be taken up in the following order: First, several factors related to the nature of the replicative study will be presented; second, the findings which supported Woodward's conclusion, those which did not, and the findings which extended Woodward's analysis will be considered; third, prospects for further research will be considered; and fourth, final reflections on the analysis will be presented.

THE REPLICATION

The Minneapolis study is not an exact replication of Woodward's work in England. Differences may be observed with respect to the samples of the firms studied, the setting of the industries included in the analysis, the quality of the data gathered, and the variables included in the analysis.

Woodward conducted a census of manufacturing firms in the southeast Essex area. She observed that while there was a fairly broad representation of industrial sectors in the sample, the newer industries, such as chemical and electronics, were somewhat overrepresented. This overrepresentation of the newer industries was reflected in the distribution of production technologies, 31 percent of the English firms studied being process production operations.

The Minneapolis sample, on the other hand, was neither a census of firms in the area nor a probability sampling of these firms. The criteria of selection of the Minneapolis firms were size of the labor force and industrial sector, data being available to allow for selection on these bases. One of the effects of the selection procedure utilized in Minneapolis was to provide a more representative coverage of industrial sectors within the sample. A further difference between the samples is that the Minneapolis sample contained a far smaller proportion of process firms, only 11 percent compared to the 31 percent in the English sample.

The socioeconomic setting of the two samples obviously differs in addition to the specific sample differences already noted.

It should also be noted that the Minneapolis data are more variable in quality than those of the English study, a function of the fact that a team of trained researchers conducted the English study while a single investigator assumed responsibility for the American study.

The general effect of these differences—sample, setting and data—is to enhance our confidence in Woodward's findings in the cases where confirmation of the English findings was observed in the Minneapolis study. The use of different data-gathering and analysis techniques increases the validity of the findings while the differences in sample and setting enhance the probable generality of the original findings.

The Minneapolis study also extended the English study by adding one independent variable, the relationship between ownership and management, and two dependent variables, the ratio of nonmanagerial supervisors to managers, and dependence of the firm on local markets.

In the majority of cases where Woodward's conclusions were tested as hypotheses there was confirmation of the English findings.

Findings Supporting Woodward

Woodward's first general finding was that there were no organizational correlates of operating success in her sample of industrial firms. This finding was confirmed in the Minneapolis study (see Chapter 2 and Appendix 3).

Woodward's second general finding was that the prescriptions on organizational structure contained in the classical management literature were specific to firms employing a large batch- or mass-production technology. This finding was confirmed in the Minneapolis study (see Chapter 3, especially Tables 6 and 7).

Woodward's third general finding was that size of the company labor force was not correlated with the organizational variables she considered in her analysis. This finding was generally confirmed in the Minneapolis study, the two specific exceptions being considered in the section dealing with findings different from those presented by Woodward.

Woodward's fourth general finding was that type of production technology was correlated with organizational characteristics. This finding was strongly supported by the Minneapolis data. Type of production technology was correlated with seven of the eight organizational variables considered in both the Essex and Minneapolis studies: span of control of the chief executive (Table 8); the ratio of workers to supervisors (Table 9); number of levels of management in the firm (Table 10); the ratio of nonproduction to production workers (Table 15ff); promotion policy of the firm (Table 17); and labor costs, (Table 18). The only exception to the Woodward's findings, with respect to the relation between technology and organization, involved the span of control of first-line supervisors.

Woodward's fifth major finding was that there were "optimum" forms of organization specific to each type of production technology, rather than a single form of optimum industrial organization. This finding was confirmed in the Minneapolis study, the data being contained in Tables 6, 7, 8, 9, 10, 15, 17, and 18; these tables indicated that the relation between organizational characteristics and technology is strongest for the very successful firms.

The general conclusion of the replication is that Woodward's findings are supported by the Minneapolis data. The exceptions are, however, worthy of note in and of themselves.

Findings Not Supporting Woodward

As noted above, size of company labor force was, in the Minneapolis study, correlated with two organizational variables, and type of production technology was not correlated with one of the organizational variables examined by Woodward.

Size of company labor force was correlated with the span of control of the chief executive (Table 11) and the number of management levels in the firm (Table 12). In the case of these two variables, it appeared as though all three of the independent variables interacted in affecting the values of these variables.

Type of production technology was very strongly related to span of control of first-line supervisors in the Essex study. It was not in any way related to type of production technology in the Minneapolis study (Appendix 4, Table 43). In fact, span of control of the first-line supervisors was in no way related to any of the independent variables and was the only organizational characteristic investigated that did not show some kind of strong relationship to one or more of the independent variables.

The exceptions to Woodward's findings are few, and only one of these contradicts her results: the lack of a relation between span of control of the first-line supervisors and type of production technology. In the case of span of control of the chief executive and the number of management levels in the firm, the relations between type of technology and these variables remains, but is complicated by the effect of the other independent variables.

Findings That Extend Woodward

The findings that represent a substantive extension of Woodward are related to the inclusion of an independent variable not considered by Woodward, the relationship between ownership and management, and the inclusion of two additional dependent variables, the ratio of nonmanagerial supervisors to managers, and dependence on local markets.

Several findings in the Minneapolis study contribute to a substantive extension of Woodward's work.

The first general finding is that the relationship between ownership and management is related to systematic variation in the values of only three of the organizational characteristics studied. Thus, while firms with separated ownership and management were more likely to have a greater number of levels of management (Table 14), a broader span of control at the top of the hierarchy (Table 13), and proportionately lower labor costs (Table 22) than were firms with combined ownership and management, the overall effect of the relationship between ownership and management on specific organizational characteristics appears to be slight.

Two of the organizational variables related to ownership and management—span of control of the chief executive and number of levels of management—were also related to technology and size of the company labor force.

In the case of the two dependent variables, which were only considered in this study, both were related to technology while only one was related to size of the labor force, and neither was related to ownership and management. The ratio of nonmanagerial supervisors to managers was correlated with type of production technology (Table 16) but not with the other independent variables. Dependence on local markets was related to both technology and size of the labor force (Tables 23, 24, and 27), but not to ownership and management.

Conclusions

The findings of the English study were rather strongly confirmed in this replication. The differences in sample and setting provide a basis for viewing the observed relationships as being generalizable to a rather wide range of industrial settings.

The research requirements now facing the student of technology and formal organization obviously point in several directions.

There is, first of all, need for refinement of the conceptualization of technology and the related research instrumentation.

There is also a need to investigate the extent to which these relationships may be generalized, both with respect to organizational and cultural settings.

Finally, there is need to consider these relationships in

the context of an open-system strategy of organizational analysis.

The overall effect of these kinds of research is to demonstrate the profound influence that the material conditions of man's life have on his social organization and to reorient the analysis of formal organization to include consideration of these important factors.

The general conclusion of this analysis is that of the three independent variables, type of production technology was most closely and consistently related to variations in the organizational characteristics of the firms, and that it was the only variable consistently related to level of business success, the relationship indicated by the strengthening of the relationships between technology and organizational characteristics when only the very successful firms were considered.

PROSPECTS

The ultimate test of a research project is its ability to generate new ideas and research. A replication and interpretation of the original English research conducted by Woodward was certainly in order at this time, particularly in a field which normally does not bother with replication. However, having reached this point it is appropriate to consider where to move in the future.

There are obviously two general approaches possible

with respect to future research. The first is to conduct more intensive survey studies of the problems posed in the original research. The second would be to conduct an extensive type of research which moves the original analysis into the context of different problems.

The most obvious direction to move in the development of more intensive studies is exploration of the possibility of turning Woodward's scale of technology into one or more precise instruments. This could take the form of either working on the scalable aspects of manufacturing technologies or integrating her typology of production technologies into more comprehensive schemes dealing with technological characteristics of organizations. This line of development would require a simultaneous concern with conceptualization and instrumentation. The outcome of successful research of this kind would be the development of standardized instruments derived from sufficiently sophisticated conceptualizations of technology to permit more detailed investigation of the relations between the technological systems of organizations and the social characteristics of these organizations.

An alternative mode of proceeding from Woodward would be to focus on an extension of the analysis into other social settings. It is ridiculous to assume that southeast Essex and Minneapolis exhaust the possible industrial complexes. Additional surveys could also accumulate valuable additional comparative data. In this case the social implications of these original analyses would be followed out and assume primacy over the technologies, per se, and related instrumentation.

Examples of interesting research prospects of an extensive nature are easy to come by. Consequently one problem, related to the general area of economic development, will be presented here as an example of the kind of extension which can be made.

There is consensus that industrialization is a requisite of large-scale economic development. The factory with its associated technology and organization must be introduced into traditional societies if affluence is to be realized in the developing regions of the world. The rate of industrialization in the developing areas is more than sufficient documentation of the fact that this process is not in any sense a simple one to initiate, nor is the ultimate goal of the creation of an industrial state one that can be assumed to be realized.

Furthermore, there is general consensus that the kinds of problems hindering the development of the industrial complex in developing states are basically social. Although the general problem of industrialization, involving the analysis of total societies and their change in form, is probably beyond the ken of contemporary social science, there are undoubtedly points at which the problem becomes manageable and provides an extraordinary field setting for the investigation of human behavior. At the level of the industrial plant the relationship between technology, social organization, and culture becomes a potentially fruitful point of entry into this complex of problems.

If a sociocultural system is in the process of change, and if this change involves the introduction of new dominant forms of social organization, then it is obvious that one of the primary questions of concern should be the relationship between the basic pattern of relations of the old forms and the new forms of organization.

Cultures probably vary as much as anthropologists say

they do in terms of the preferred patterns of relationships institutionalized. What this research suggests is that the desired patterns of relationship within the industrial complex also varies considerably, and that the key to the variation within the industrial firms is the production technology. Thus it becomes more than reasonable to begin investigating the possibility that a particularly effective way of approaching the problem of industrialization would be to try to match, insofar as possible, traditional patterns of relationships with those possible in the industrial firm by the judicious selection of the appropriate form of production technology.

The extension of this research into the area of industrialization draws the analysis into a significant consideration of general milieu variables, and focuses analysis on the dynamics of organizational behavior.

The extension of this approach into other institutional settings is obviously possible, there being nothing in the general argument which is specific to manufacturing operations.

THE WIDER SOCIAL MILIEU

If we return for the moment to the broad findings in the replication on Minneapolis data of Woodward's study of industrial southeast Essex, the movement beyond her study to a consideration of the market and wider social milieu is not difficult to rationalize.

Although the replication of the Woodward study supported the basic findings reported in the Essex analysis, there were differences, with respect both to the frequency distribution of values of some of the variables (e.g., a greater proportion of supervisory personnel generally present among the Minneapolis firms than was reported in the Essex study), and to the relationship between the type of production system utilized and the values of organizational characteristics (the reporting of a strong relationship between the average span of control of first-line supervisors and technology in the Essex study and the absence of such a relationship in the Minneapolis replication).

The attempt to explain the differences between the English and American data led us to explore three variables not included in the Essex study: the ratio of nonmanagerial supervisors to managers (an organization variable), and dependency on local or nonlocal markets for the acquisition of production materials and/or sales (market variables). This extension can be seen as adding additional confirmation to Woodward's findings along the general direction she had indicated. However, differences still remain to be accounted for. Among these are: (1) the relatively greater proportion of supervisory to nonsupervisory personnel present in the Minneapolis than in the Essex sample; (2) the absence of a relationship between production technology and span of control of first-line supervisor in the Minneapolis sample; and, most striking of all, (3) the general lack in the Minneapolis data of as sharply a drawn line between success and failure of the industrial enterprise as appears in the Essex industries.

The question could be posed as to how best to proceed

to account for these residual differences. Since in classical theory the market is the point of contact between economic productive activities and the wider society, one could potentially expand one's conception of its components. However, since the Marxian theory seeks to utilize a variety of nonmarket devices (such as decisions by politically established commissars of bureaus) for the allocation of economic resources, one could consider the broader social milieu as comprising a class of variables affecting the economic process over and beyond the market proper.

The marketplace of Marxian and classical economic thought was the institution where a number of independent producers could interact in a struggle for possession of limited economic resources. The competition was conceived in contemporary terms as a zero-sum game where victory could be attained only at the expense of other players. In classical economic theory the losers and victors were variably efficient industries, whereas in Marxian analysis workers were the losers and the capitalists the victors.

The market so conceived promoted economic rationality. Those competitors who were most rational, scientific, expedient and ruthless would survive at the expense of the weak, irrational, and inefficient.

However, circumstances could be quite different in a market economy in which conditions of comparative abundance rather than scarcity of economic resources—including labor—is the rule. Theory and research strategy could treat the comparative scarcity or abundance in the general system of economic life either as general conditions of the market or as properties of the wider milieu. Here for the moment, as a basis for sharpening discussion, the second alternative is pursued, but the basic analysis would not be substantially changed if affluence and its lack were conceived as characteristics of the market. In either case, it is our thesis that what constitutes "rational" market behavior will be different in a nonaffluent and an affluent society.

The contemporary English economy does, in certain critical respects, approximate the classical model of the market. Because of the historical location of the British economy the relevant markets are of worldwide scope rather than national or local. However, it is also true that the major English industries are backed to the wall in their struggle for a place in the sun. This is particularly the case for the newer industries represented in Woodward's study by chemicals, electronics, oil, and aircraft industries. The concern with the well-being, or lack thereof, of these English industries is constantly paraded before the public. Their competitive position is severely weakened by the lack of certain critical resources, such as raw materials, a tight labor situation which seriously constrains the opportunities of management to innovate easily and effectively, and the age-old traditions which seem a part of every English institution and ideology. Under these circumstances the organization of the firm is particularly critical as the one aspect whose rationalization is available to management in its response to competition. Furthermore, this alternative is the one property most readily available for manipulation in English society, at the time of the opening of new plants or operations,[1] or the introduction of new technologies, since this is a time of maximal administrative control and minimal market certainty—the most opportune situation in which social innovation can be introduced at the top. Southeast Essex then, is an area where English management has had considerable opportunity to respond innovatively by rationalization of industrial organizations.

The need for efficiency, coupled with the opportunity for rationalization, would under such circumstances be expected to produce an organizational structure rather closely keyed to the needs of productions technology.

The Minneapolis industries, on the other hand, thrive in an affluent socioeconomic milieu which provides management with greater discretionary powers than is possible for English management. Minneapolis industries are less constrained by traditions as well as less bitterly competitive. The administration of Minneapolis industry enjoys far greater opportunities for innovation at a variety of points in industrial operations.

The affluent Minneapolis milieu permits management to choose among a number of possibilities related to rationalization of the industrial operation; rationalization of the organizational structure is only one of these alternatives. It is much easier for administrators to indulge personal preference with respect to the reorganization of the firm. Furthermore, under benign economic circumstances, individuals have a much greater opportunity to reward one another generously, with respect to status and authority, position, and remuneration.

One result of these differences in socioeconomic milieu can be stated. Under conditions of affluence, economic expansion, and a lack of serious economic competition (threat to organizational survival), administrators—on the basis of their personal preferences and out of a situation of negotiation with employees—freely utilize a reward system which involves a dramatic increase in the number of supervisory positions within the organization. The constraints operative on the English system force economy and the reduction of supervisory positions. The American affluence also has the effect of reducing the proportion of employees engaged in direct production activities. The fact that a relation is still observed between these variables and type of production system in the Minneapolis setting thus provides especially strong support for the argument that technology is a major organizational determinant.

The relationship betwen span of control of first-line supervisor and technology reveals that under affluent socio-economic circumstances various organizational properties may be manipulated according to purely social demands made by relevant individuals or collectivities, administrators, or even unions.

One implication of the role of the milieu in the English and the Minneapolis studies is that men have much less discretionary control over industrial organizations than is generally assumed by the human-relations approach to industrial organization. At the same time the variations found between the English and midwestern samples strongly bring into question the notion that technology and market demands always overwhelm the administrator in such a way as to preclude decisions based on ideological preferences—whether these preferences be radical, liberal, or conservative. In any case, in the empirical studies of the relations between industrial organization, technology, and a variety of other variables in southeast Essex and the midwestern United

States, the approaches to organization growing out of the Marxian and classical economic theories were brought into confrontation. The forced confrontation between the Marxian and classical perspectives has produced a number of important insights into the area of organization theory.

First, the critical elements in both the Marxian and the classical traditions must be combined into a new approach for the analysis of organization theory. This includes a consideration of both the materialism and the conflict perspectives[2] of Marx and the decisional and milieu concerns[3] of the classical tradition. Intellectual traditions which persist through time normally contain basic insights which are ignored only at peril to the analysis.

Second, perspectives focusing on only one level of analysis are inadequate. Perhaps the greatest failing in the human relations tradition is its exclusive concern with trying to explain behavior within organizations on the basis of an elaborated exchange theory.

Third, a recognition of the need for a more sophisticated conceptual approach to the analysis of complex organizations demands that we move from a heavy reliance upon the case study method to a greater reliance upon the general survey method.

Finally, there is a crying need for greater continuity in research efforts. Ultimately the validation of proposed research findings rests upon some form of research replication. The entire history of the empirical sciences is built upon this continuity, and a lingering obsession with completely novel research can only prolong the confusion currently characterizing organization theory.

NOTES

1. For a very important discussion of the limitations placed upon administrative innovation in a constrained social milieu and of the importance of new construction and renovation as opportunities for social innovation, see Michael Crozier, *The Bureaucratic Phenomenon* (Chicago: University of Chicago Press, 1964).

2. For an interesting discussion of the importance of material conditions on industrial organization which relates to a consideration of production technology, see William A. Rushing, "Hardness of Material as Related to Division of Labor in Manufacturing Industries," *Administrative Science Quarterly* 13 (September, 1968): 229–245. Two unique discussions of conflict as a variable central to the analysis of organization are found in: Melville Dalton, *Men Who Manage* (New York: John Wiley & Sons, 1959); and Sherman Krupp, *Pattern in Organization Analysis: A Critical Examination* (New York: Holt, Rinehart and Winston, 1961).

3. A concern with decision-making and execution is, of course, a dominant focus of analysis in the business management and human relations literature. It is also one of the key focuses of the new works in systems management. Studies of the relationship between organizations and their milieus are relatively rare because of the research complications posed by simultaneous consideration of organizational and milieu variables. References to the need for an open system strategy of analysis and traditional lip service paid to the need for consideration of cultural variables, are more than sufficient indicators that these factors have long been recognized as important for a full understanding of organizational structure and processes.

APPENDIXES

APPENDIX 1

THE QUESTIONNAIRE

The data from the Minneapolis industrial-commercial area were gathered by questionnaire. Since the purpose of the study was primarily intended to replicate Woodward's study, the questions were modeled on hers. The major difference between the two studies, with respect to the questionnaire, was that the Minneapolis instrument was more simply conceived in order to permit the use of interviewers who were not as well trained, or as experienced, as those employed by Woodward. In a few instances data not gathered by Woodward were included in the Minneapolis study, and some data gathered in the English study were omitted.

Had an attempt been made to work with the scale of technological complexity developed by Woodward, it would then have been necessary to test this questionnaire for reliability and validity. The decision to work with the threefold typology of industrial production systems made this unnecessary.

QUESTIONNAIRE

<u>Name</u> <u>of</u> <u>Firm</u>:
<u>Location</u>:
<u>Name</u> <u>and</u> <u>Position</u> <u>of</u> <u>Person</u> <u>Interviewed</u>:

Product Information

Product:*

Product	Percent of total production
_____	_____
_____	_____
_____	_____
_____	_____
_____	_____
_____	_____
_____	_____
_____	_____
_____	_____
_____	_____

* If there are a very large number of specific items manufactured it may be necessary to group these on the basis of the similarity of the products and the process utilized in their manufacture.

Form A

Fill out a form A for each major product (or type of product).

Product: _____

_____ component
_____ complete item
_____ product manufactured to customer's specification
_____ product manufactured to company specifications
_____ product manufactured in single units
_____ small batches
_____ large batches
_____ manufactured on assembly-line basis (fixed assembly line with staging operations)
_____ product mass produced
_____ continuous production of liquid, gas, or solid
_____ combination of the above (specify) _____

Number of stages in the production process _____

_____ product sold directly to person or organization using it
_____ product sold to distributor

Value of product: _____ (actual cash value if available)

      _____ very great
      _____ considerable
      _____ modest
      _____ inexpensive

Capital value of industrial plant, including equipment: _____ (actual cash value if available)

      _____ major capital investment
      _____ considerable capital investment

The Questionnaire

_____ moderate capital investment
_____ relatively small capital investment

Organization of Firm

Headquarters
_____ local
_____ outside Twin City area

Operation
_____ locally centered operation
_____ dispersed operation (also outside of Twin Cities)

Relation of Ownership to Management
_____ combined ownership and management
_____ separated ownership and management

Suppliers of production materials
_____ predominantly local
_____ mostly local
_____ considerably local
_____ little local

Markets
_____ predominantly local
_____ mostly local
_____ considerably local
_____ little local

Advancement policy
_____ promote from within
_____ fill administrative vacancies with persons from the outside
_____ mixed

Obtain an organizational chart of the firm (if one is not available draw one up)

Number of authority levels in firm's hierarchy_____

Flexibility of decision-making structure and lines of communication.

Extent of research and development activities

Labor Characteristics

_____ total number of employees
number of salaried workers _____
number of wage workers _____
other (specify) _____
_____ number of production workers
_____ number of maintenance workers
_____ number of clerical workers
_____ number of administrative employees
    _____ managers
    _____ supervisors
    _____ first-line supervisors (foremen)
_____ other (specify) _____

Operating costs
   labor _____
   materials _____
   other _____ (specify if possible) _____

Brief History of the Firm

Success of Firm's Operation

APPENDIX 2

SOME METHODOLOGICAL CONSIDERATIONS

Inasmuch as the present study was a replication of Woodward's, there were no special procedural problems with respect to basic research instruments other than insuring that ones comparable to those employed by Woodward were used. There were, however, three problems which could potentially affect the value of the replication: character of the sample, procedures followed in gathering data, and analysis. Each could potentially affect the comparability of the two studies.

The Sample

The analysis was based on data collected from 63 firms in the Twin City metropolitan area. The Essex sample consisted of 100 firms, 91 percent of all firms in the area with a labor force of 100 or greater. The Essex firms covered a wide range of industrial sectors but were concentrated in areas of recent industrial development, e.g., electronics and chemicals. The Essex firms also tended to be relatively new, consistent with the late industrialization of the area. Unfortunately, the author does not provide data on the distribution of firms by industrial sector.

A census approach was impossible in the case of the Minneapolis sample. There are approximately 2,400 manufacturing firms in the five-county metropolitan area of Minneapolis and St. Paul. The sample finally selected was not representative of industry in this area. If, however, the posited relationships are valid they should be found throughout the industrial complex.

The major differences between the Essex and Minneapolis samples are listed here. First, the Minneapolis sample is more representative of the various industrial sectors containing manufacturing firms. The 55 firms included in the data analysis were drawn from 18 of the major industrial sectors used in the Standard Industrial Classification of firms; a majority of the sectors included manufacturing firms.

Second, the Minneapolis industrial complex has grown up over a period of a hundred years, creating a mix of types and ages of industries. The Essex industrial development, on the other hand, is more homogeneous with respect to both age and type of industry.

Finally, as noted above, the Minneapolis sample is

neither a census of manufacturing firms nor a probability sample of these firms, whereas the Essex sample is a near census of the larger firms in the area.

Data Gathering

Data for the Minneapolis replication were gathered during June and July 1966. The information was obtained by student assistants, trained by the researcher, in interviews with managerial personnel of the firms. The Essex study employed a team of experienced researchers over an extended period of time.

The amount and range of information collected by the Essex team could not be duplicated in the Minneapolis setting. Moreover, the reliability of the Essex data is potentially greater than for the Minneapolis study. Since the general effect of experience is to increase the consistence of observation and recording, the Minneapolis findings are the more impressive. It is not unfair to guess that our study underestimates the extent of replication rather than overestimating it.

The interviews varied in length from 15 minutes to three hours, with the majority requiring about 45 minutes. The cooperation of management was excellent. Sixty-nine firms were contacted. Only two firms refused to cooperate, and the administration in one other firm delayed the interview long enough to force the selection of another firm. In three cases the interviewers were admitted but unable to obtain sufficient usable data for inclusion in the study.

Usable data, then, were obtained on 63 of the 69 firms, a proportion comparing favorably with the Essex case, where Woodward and her associates were able to gain entrance to

100 of the 110 firms contacted. Eight of the 63 firms surveyed employed labor forces of less than 100 and were dropped from the final analysis.

While no systematic check on interviewer reliability was possible, several steps were taken to provide an idea of the reliability of the data gathered. First, one of the firms included in the study was investigated more intensely and no discrepancies were observed—a firm in which the original interviewer had not been able to establish good rapport with the manager interviewed.

Second, an examination of published materials relating to some of the firms was conducted, particularly those relating to the question of operating success, and no discrepancies were observed.

Third, an independent study of two firms not included within the sample was conducted to obtain a better idea of the problems the interviewers might have encountered in their attempts to acquire various types of information. The results of this inquiry indicated that the data gathered by the interviewers, with the reservations they noted, appeared to be adequate for the analysis.

These informal checks on interviewer reliability coupled with the comments of the interviewers all indicated that the data were adequate for the task, despite the fact it was not as "clean" as that utilized in the Essex study.

Analysis

In the original study of industrial organization and technology Woodward created a scale of industrial production technologies, ranging them from the simplest of manufacturing technology to the most complex. Her analysis, however, utilized a simple typology of three types of production technologies, unit and small-batch production, large-batch and mass-production, and process production. This analysis utilizes the typology presented by Woodward, in keeping with the form of her analysis.

The data analysis of Woodward consisted of the presentation of the raw data accompanied by median values for the various frequency distributions. The present analysis relies primarily upon the presentation of the raw data in standardized form, percentages, with accompanying median values when these are appropriate. Being a replication study, it maintains the necessary consistency with the original analysis while avoiding some of the problems associated with the reading of raw data.

In addition to the simple presentation of results, some chi-squares are presented for the tables when these seem appropriate. The sample procedure does not technically warrant these but they are presented when possible to provide the reader with a rough indication of the significance of association between variables. The guide utilized in determining when a chi-square is presented is the complexity of the table being considered. With a sample of only 55 it seems unwarranted to compute a test of significance on a very complex table: in this case values are computed for tables with six or fewer cells.

APPENDIX 3

SUPPLEMENTAL TABLES FOR CHAPTER 2

TABLE 29

DISTRIBUTION OF PRODUCTION TECHNOLOGIES IN MINNEAPOLIS AND ESSEX SAMPLES

TECHNOLOGY	SAMPLE			
	Minneapolis		Essex	
	No.	%	No.	%
Unit and Small-Batch				
I. Production of units to customers' requirements	1	2	5	6
II. Production of prototypes	2	4	10	12
III. Fabrication of large equipment in stages	5	9	2	2
VI. Production of small batches to customers' orders	11	20	7	9
Subtotal	19	35	24	29
Large-Batch and Mass				
V. Production of large batches	8	15	14	18
VI. Production of large batches on assembly line	18	33	11	14
VII. Mass production	4	7	6	8
Subtotal	30	55	31	40
Process				
VIII. Intermittent production of chemicals in multipurpose plant	3	5	13	16
IX. Continuous flow production of liquids, gases, and crystalline substances	3	5	12	15
Subtotal	6	10	25	31
Total	55	100	80	100

TABLE 30

PRODUCTION TECHNOLOGY, SIZE OF LABOR FORCE, AND LEVEL OF BUSINESS SUCCESS IN MINNEAPOLIS FIRMS

	TECHNOLOGY											
	UNIT AND SMALL-BATCH Size of Labor Force				LARGE-BATCH AND MASS Size of Labor Force				PROCESS Size of Labor Force			
	1,000 or less		More than 1,000		1,000 or less		More than 1,000		1,000 or less		More than 1,000	
LEVEL OF SUCCESS	No.	%	No.	%	No.	%	No.	%	No.	%	No.	%
Very successful	6	43	4	80	7	39	8	67	3	100	3	100
Less successful	8	57	1	20	11	61	4	33	—	—	—	—
Total	14	100	5	100	18	100	12	100	3	100	3	100

TABLE 31

SEPARATION OF OWNERSHIP AND MANAGEMENT, AND LEVEL OF BUSINESS SUCCESS IN SMALLER MINNEAPOLIS FIRMS[a]

LEVEL OF SUCCESS	OWNERSHIP AND MANAGEMENT[b]			
	Combined		Separated	
	No.	%	No.	%
Very successful	6	37	10	53
Less successful	10	63	9	47
Total	16	100	19	100

[a] Firms with 1,000 or fewer employees
[b] $\chi^2 = 0.846$ (df = 1), $p > .30$.

TABLE 32

TYPE OF MANAGEMENT SYSTEM AND LEVEL OF BUSINESS SUCCESS IN MINNEAPOLIS FIRMS

LEVEL OF SUCCESS	TYPE OF MANAGEMENT SYSTEM[a]			
	Organic		Mechanical	
	No.	%	No.	%
Very successful	15	54	12	67
Less successful	13	46	6	33
Total	28	100	18	100

[a] $\chi^2 = 0.775$ (df = 1), $p > .30$.

APPENDIX 3

TABLE 33

NUMBER OF LEVELS OF MANAGEMENT HIERARCHY AND LEVEL OF BUSINESS SUCCESS IN MINNEAPOLIS FIRMS

NUMBER OF LEVELS OF MANAGEMENT HIERARCHY	LEVEL OF SUCCESS					
	Very Successful		Less Successful		Total	
	No.	%	No.	%	No.	%
3	4	13	5	21	9	17
4	5	17	7	29	12	22
5	9	30	6	25	15	28
6	9	30	5	21	14	26
7	3	10	—	—	13	6
8	—	—	1	4	1	2
Total	30	100	24	100	64	101
Median	5		4.5		5	

Supplemental Tables for Chapter 2

TABLE 34

SPAN OF CONTROL OF CHIEF EXECUTIVE AND LEVEL OF BUSINESS SUCCESS IN MINNEAPOLIS FIRMS

SPAN OF CONTROL	LEVEL OF SUCCESS					
	Very Successful		Less Successful		Total	
	No.	%	No.	%	No.	%
1	—	—	1	4	1	2
2	1	3	—	—	1	2
3	2	7	4	17	6	11
4	8	27	3	12	11	21
5	3	10	3	12	6	11
6	3	10	6	25	9	17
7	1	3	4	17	5	9
8	2	7	1	4	3	6
9	3	10	2	8	5	9
10	1	3	—	—	1	2
11 or more	6	20	—	—	6	11
Total	30	100	24	99	54	101
Median	6		6		6	

TABLE 35

SPAN OF CONTROL OF FIRST-LINE SUPERVISOR AND LEVEL OF BUSINESS SUCCESS IN MINNEAPOLIS FIRMS

SPAN OF CONTROL	LEVEL OF SUCCESS					
	Very Successful		Less Successful		Total	
	No	%	No	%	No.	%
1–5	1	4	—	—	1	2
6–10	4	15	1	4	5	10
11–15	3	12	6	26	9	18
16–20	8	31	6	26	14	29
21–25	—	—	2	9	2	4
26–30	1	4	—	—	1	2
31–35	6	23	6	26	12	24
36–40	1	4	—	—	1	2
41–45	—	—	—	—	—	—
46–50	1	4	1	4	2	4
51 or more	1	4	1	4	2	4
Total	26	101	23	99	49	99
Median	19.5		20		20	

Supplemental Tables for Chapter 2

TABLE 36

RATIO OF NONSUPERVISORY PERSONNEL TO SUPERVISORS AND LEVEL OF BUSINESS SUCCESS IN MINNEAPOLIS FIRMS

NUMBER OF NON-SUPERVISORS FOR EACH SUPERVISOR	LEVEL OF SUCCESS					
	Very Successful		Less Successful		Total	
	No.	%	No.	%	No.	%
3 or less	1	4	1	4	2	4
4	3	11	—	—	3	6
5	4	14	2	9	6	12
6	3	11	1	4	4	8
7	1	4	—	—	1	2
8	2	7	1	4	3	6
9	3	11	3	12	6	12
10	—	—	1	4	1	2
11	1	4	2	9	3	6
12	1	4	—	—	1	2
13	—	—	3	12	3	6
14	2	7	1	4	3	6
15	1	4	2	9	3	6
16 or more	6	21	7	29	13	25
Total	28	102	24	100	52	101
Median	8.5		13		10.5	

TABLE 37

RATIO OF PRODUCTION TO NONPRODUCTION WORKERS AND LEVEL OF BUSINESS SUCCESS IN MINNEAPOLIS FIRMS

NUMBER OF PRODUCTION WORKERS FOR EACH NONPRODUCTION WORKER	LEVEL OF SUCCESS					
	Very Successful		Less Successful		Total	
	No.	%	No.	%	No.	%
Less than 1	10	32	—	—	10	18
1	2	6	2	8	4	8
2	7	23	9	39	16	29
3	5	16	2	8	7	13
4	3	10	4	17	7	13
5	1	3	2	8	3	6
6	—	—	1	4	1	2
7 or more	3	10	4	17	7	13
Total	31	100	24	101	55	102
Median	2		3		2	

TABLE 38

RATIO OF NONMANAGERIAL SUPERVISORS TO MANAGERS AND LEVEL OF BUSINESS SUCCESS IN MINNEAPOLIS FIRMS

NUMBER OF NON-MANAGERIAL SUPERVISORS FOR EACH MANAGER	LEVEL OF SUCCESS					
	Very Successful		Less Successful		Total	
	No.	%	No.	%	No.	%
Less than 1	5	18	7	29	12	24
1	1	4	2	8	3	6
2	7	26	6	25	13	25
3	2	6	—	—	2	4
4	4	15	6	25	10	20
5	1	4	1	4	2	4
6	—	—	—	—	—	—
7	—	—	1	4	1	2
8	1	4	—	—	1	2
9	—	—	—	—	—	—
10	1	4	—	—	1	2
11	1	4	—	—	1	2
12 or more	4	15	1	4	5	10
Total	27	100	24	99	51	101
Median	2		2		2	

TABLE 39

LABOR COSTS AND LEVEL OF BUSINESS SUCCESS IN MINNEAPOLIS FIRMS

LABOR COSTS—PERCENTAGE OF OPERATING COSTS	LEVEL OF SUCCESS					
	Very Successful		Less Successful		Total	
	No.	%	No.	%	No.	%
Less than 12.5 percent	1	4	3	21	4	12
21.5–25	7	29	—	—	7	18
26–50	11	46	7	50	18	47
51 or more	5	21	4	29	9	24
Total	24	100	14	100	38	101
Median	30		39		33	

TABLE 40

PROMOTION POLICY AND LEVEL OF BUSINESS SUCCESS IN MINNEAPOLIS FIRMS

LEVEL OF SUCCESS	PROMOTION POLICY[a]			
	Promote from Within		Mixed	
	No.	%	No.	%
Very successful	22	61	9	47
Less successful	14	39	10	53
Total	36	100	19	100

[a] $\chi^2 = 0.963$ (df = 1), $p > .30$.

TABLE 41

DEPENDENCE UPON LOCAL MARKETS FOR PRODUCTION SUPPLIES AND LEVEL OF BUSINESS SUCCESS IN MINNEAPOLIS FIRMS

LEVEL OF SUCCESS	DEPENDENCE UPON LOCAL MARKETS FOR PRODUCTION SUPPLIES[a]			
	Considerable		Little or None	
	No.	%	No.	%
Very successful	16	57	15	56
Less successful	12	43	12	44
Total	28	100	27	100

[a] $\chi^2 = 0.025$ (df = 1), $p > .80$.

TABLE 42

DEPENDENCE UPON LOCAL MARKETS FOR SALES AND LEVEL OF BUSINESS SUCCESS IN MINNEAPOLIS FIRMS

LEVEL OF SUCCESS	DEPENDENCE UPON LOCAL MARKETS FOR SALES[a]			
	Considerable		Little or None	
	No.	%	No.	%
Very successful	13	59	18	55
Less successful	9	41	15	45
Total	22	100	33	100

[a] $\chi^2 = 0.111$ (df = 1), $p > .70$.

APPENDIX 4

SUPPLEMENTAL TABLES FOR CHAPTER 4

TABLE 43

PRODUCTION TECHNOLOGY, SPAN OF CONTROL OF FIRST-LINE SUPERVISORS, AND LEVEL OF BUSINESS SUCCESS IN MINNEAPOLIS FIRMS

LEVEL OF SUCCESS AND SPAN OF CONTROL	TECHNOLOGY					
	Unit and Small-Batch		Large-Batch and Mass		Process	
	No.	%	No.	%	No.	%
All Firms						
1–5	—	—	—	—	1	25
6–10	2	12	3	11	—	—
11–15	4	24	5	18	—	—
16–20	4	24	8	28	2	50
21–25	—	—	2	7	—	—
26–30	—	—	1	4	—	—
31–35	6	35	5	18	1	25
36–40	1	6	—	—	—	—
41–45	—	—	—	—	—	—
46–50	—	—	2	7	—	—
51 or more	—	—	2	7	—	—
Total	17	101	28	100	4	100
Median	20		19.8		16.8	
Very Successful Firms						
1–5	—	—	—	—	1	25
6–10	2	22	2	15	—	—
11–15	2	22	1	8	—	—
16–20	2	22	4	31	2	50
21–25	—	—	—	—	—	—
26–30	—	—	1	8	—	—
31–35	2	22	3	23	1	25
36–40	1	11	—	—	—	—
41–45	—	—	—	—	—	—
46–50	—	—	1	8	—	—
51 or more	—	—	1	8	—	—
Total	9	99	13	101	4	100
Median	19		20		16.8	

TABLE 44

SIZE OF LABOR FORCE, SPAN OF CONTROL OF FIRST-LINE SUPERVISORS, AND LEVEL OF BUSINESS SUCCESS IN MINNEAPOLIS FIRMS

LEVEL OF SUCCESS AND SPAN OF CONTROL	SIZE OF LABOR FORCE			
	1,000 or less		More than 1,000	
	No.	%	No.	%
All Firms				
1–5	1	3	—	—
6–10	3	9	2	13
11–15	6	17	3	20
16–20	10	29	4	27
21–25	1	3	2	13
26–30	—	—	2	13
31–35	10	29	—	—
36–40	1	3	—	—
41–45	—	—	—	—
46–50	1	3	1	7
51 or more	1	3	1	7
Total	34	99	15	100
Median	20		18.3	
Very Successful Firms				
1–5	1	6	—	—
6–10	2	12	2	20
11–15	3	19	—	—
16–20	5	31	3	30
21–25	—	—	—	—
26–30	—	—	1	10
31–35	4	25	2	20
36–40	1	6	—	—
41–45	—	—	—	—
46–50	—	—	1	10
51 or more	—	—	1	10
Total	16	99	10	100
Median	20		23.5	

TABLE 45

SIZE OF LABOR FORCE, RATIO OF NONSUPERVISORY TO SUPERVISORY PERSONNEL, AND LEVEL OF BUSINESS SUCCESS IN MINNEAPOLIS FIRMS

LEVEL OF SUCCESS AND NUMBER OF NONSUPERVISORS FOR EACH SUPERVISOR	SIZE OF LABOR FORCE			
	1,000 or less		More than 1,000	
	No.	%	No.	%
All Firms				
3 or less	1	3	1	6
4	3	9	—	—
5	4	11	2	12
6	1	3	3	18
7	—	—	1	6
8	3	9	—	—
9	4	11	2	12
10	1	3	—	—
11	2	6	1	6
12	—	—	1	6
13	3	9	—	—
14	2	6	1	6
15	2	6	1	6
16 or more	9	26	4	24
Total	35	102	17	102
Median	11		9	

TABLE 45 (continued)

LEVEL OF SUCCESS AND NUMBER OF NONSUPERVISORS FOR EACH SUPERVISOR	SIZE OF LABOR FORCE			
	1,000 or less		More than 1,000	
	No.	%	No.	%
Very Successful Firms				
3 or less	—	—	1	8
4	3	19	—	—
5	3	19	1	8
6	1	6	2	17
7	—	—	1	8
8	2	12	—	—
9	2	12	1	8
10	—	—	—	—
11	1	6	—	—
12	—	—	1	8
13	—	—	—	—
14	1	6	1	8
15	1	6	—	—
16 or more	2	12	4	33
Total	16	98	12	98
Median	8		10.5	

TABLE 46

SEPARATION OF OWNERSHIP AND MANAGEMENT, SPAN OF CONTROL OF FIRST-LINE SUPERVISORS, AND LEVEL OF BUSINESS SUCCESS IN MINNEAPOLIS FIRMS

LEVEL OF SUCCESS AND SPAN OF CONTROL	OWNERSHIP AND MANAGEMENT			
	Combined		Separated	
	No.	%	No.	%
All Firms				
1–5	—	—	1	3
6–10	1	7	4	12
11–15	3	20	6	18
16–20	4	27	10	29
21–25	—	—	2	6
26–30	—	—	1	3
31–35	5	33	7	21
36–40	1	7	—	—
41–45	—	—	—	—
46–50	—	—	2	6
51 or more	1	7	1	3
Total	15	101	34	101
Median	20.0		19.3	
Very Successful Firms				
1–5	—	—	1	5
6–10	—	—	4	20
11–15	2	33	1	5
16–20	2	33	6	30
21–25	—	—	—	—
26–30	—	—	1	5
31–35	1	16	5	25
36–40	1	16	—	—
41–45	—	—	—	—
46–50	—	—	1	5
51 or more	—	—	1	5
Total	6	98	20	100
Median	18.4		19.5	

TABLE 47

SEPARATION OF OWNERSHIP AND MANAGEMENT, RATIO OF NONSUPERVISORY TO SUPERVISORY PERSONNEL, AND LEVEL OF BUSINESS SUCCESS IN MINNEAPOLIS FIRMS

LEVEL OF SUCCESS AND NUMBER OF NONSUPERVISORS FOR EACH SUPERVISOR	OWNERSHIP AND MANAGEMENT			
	Combined		Separated	
	No.	%	No.	%
All Firms				
3 or less	1	6	1	3
4	1	6	2	6
5	—	—	6	17
6	1	6	3	8
7	—	—	1	3
8	1	6	2	6
9	2	13	4	11
10	—	—	1	3
11	2	13	1	3
12	—	—	1	3
13	1	6	2	6
14	2	13	1	3
15	—	—	3	8
16 or more	5	31	8	22
Total	16	100	36	102
Median	12		9	

TABLE 47 (continued)

LEVEL OF SUCCESS AND NUMBER OF NONSUPERVISORS FOR EACH SUPERVISOR	OWNERSHIP AND MANAGEMENT			
	Combined		Separated	
	No.	%	No.	%
Very Successful Firms				
3 or less	—	—	1	5
4	1	17	2	9
5	—	—	4	18
6	1	17	2	9
7	—	—	1	5
8	1	17	1	5
9	1	17	2	9
10	—	—	—	—
11	1	17	—	—
12	—	—	1	5
13	—	—	—	—
14	1	17	1	5
15	—	—	1	5
16 or more	—	—	6	27
Total	6	102	22	102
Median	8.5		8.5	

APPENDIX 5

SUPPLEMENTAL TABLES FOR CHAPTER 5

TABLE 48

SIZE OF LABOR FORCE, RATIO OF PRODUCTION TO NONPRODUCTION WORKERS, AND LEVEL OF BUSINESS SUCCESS IN MINNEAPOLIS FIRMS

LEVEL OF SUCCESS AND NUMBER OF PRODUCTION WORKERS FOR EACH NON-PRODUCTION WORKER	SIZE OF LABOR FORCE			
	1,000 or less		More than 1,000	
	No.	%	No.	%
All Firms				
0.5	5	14	5	25
1	1	3	3	15
2	11	31	6	30
3	3	9	3	15
4	9	26	—	—
5	1	3	—	—
6	2	6	—	—
7	1	3	1	5
8	—	—	1	5
9 or more	2	6	1	5
Total	35	101	20	100
Median	3		2	
Very Successful Firms				
0.5	5	31	5	33
1	—	—	2	13
2	5	31	2	13
3	2	12	3	20
4	4	25	—	—
5	—	—	—	—
6	—	—	—	—
7	—	—	1	7
8	—	—	1	7
9 or more	—	—	1	7
Total	16	99	15	100
Median	2		2	

TABLE 49

SIZE OF LABOR FORCE, RATIO OF SUPERVISORS TO MANAGERS, AND LEVEL OF BUSINESS SUCCESS IN MINNEAPOLIS FIRMS

LEVEL OF SUCCESS AND NUMBER OF SUPERVISORS FOR EACH MANAGER	SIZE OF LABOR FORCE			
	1,000 or less		More than 1,000	
	No.	%	No.	%
All Firms				
Less than 1	12	34	—	—
1	2	6	1	6
2	10	29	3	19
3	—	—	2	12
4	5	14	5	31
5	2	6	—	—
6	—	—	—	—
7	1	3	—	—
8	—	—	1	6
9	—	—	—	—
10	1	3	—	—
11 or more	2	6	4	25
Total	35	101	16	99
Median	2		4	
Very Successful Firms				
Less than 1	5	31	—	—
1	—	—	1	9
2	5	31	2	18
3	—	—	2	18
4	2	12	2	18
5	1	6	—	—
6	—	—	—	—
7	—	—	—	—
8	—	—	1	9
9	—	—	—	—
10	1	6	—	—
11 or more	2	12	3	27
Total	16	98	11	99
Median	2		4	

TABLE 50

SIZE OF LABOR FORCE, PROMOTION POLICY, AND LEVEL OF BUSINESS SUCCESS IN MINNEAPOLIS FIRMS

LEVEL OF SUCCESS AND PROMOTION POLICY	SIZE OF LABOR FORCE			
	1,000 or less		More than 1,000	
	No.	%	No.	%
All Firms				
Advance from within	22	63	14	70
Mixed	13	37	6	30
Total	35	100	20	100
Very Successful Firms				
Advance from within	10	62	12	80
Mixed	6	38	3	20
Total	16	100	15	100

APPENDIX 6

SUPPLEMENTAL TABLES FOR CHAPTER 6

TABLE 51

SEPARATION OF OWNERSHIP AND MANAGEMENT, DEPENDENCE UPON LOCAL MARKETS FOR PRODUCTION SUPPLIES, AND LEVEL OF BUSINESS SUCCESS IN MINNEAPOLIS FIRMS

LEVEL OF BUSINESS SUCCESS AND DEPENDENCE UPON LOCAL MARKETS FOR PRODUCTION SUPPLIES	OWNERSHIP AND MANAGEMENT			
	Combined		Separated	
	No.	%	No.	%
All Firms				
Considerably dependent	8	50	20	51
Little or no dependence	8	50	19	49
Total	16	100	39	100
Very Successful Firms				
Considerably dependent	5	83	11	44
Little or no dependence	1	17	14	56
Total	6	100	25	100

TABLE 52

SEPARATION OF OWNERSHIP AND MANAGEMENT, DEPENDENCE UPON LOCAL MARKETS FOR SALES, AND LEVEL OF BUSINESS SUCCESS IN MINNEAPOLIS FIRMS

LEVEL OF BUSINESS SUCCESS AND DEPENDENCE UPON LOCAL MARKETS FOR SALES	OWNERSHIP AND MANAGEMENT			
	Combined		Separated	
	No.	%	No.	%
All Firms				
Considerably dependent	6	38	16	41
Little or no dependence	10	62	23	59
Total	16	100	39	100
Very Successful Firms				
Considerably dependent	3	50	10	40
Little or no dependence	3	50	15	60
Total	6	100	25	100

Supplemental Tables for Chapter 6

APPENDIX 7

EVALUATION OF OPERATING SUCCESS

The categorization of firms into those that were very successful and those that were less successful was based on a number of considerations. One question that does arise in such a classification relates to the reliability of the classification. The following material is presented to allow the reader to make his own judgment regarding reliability.

The question of validity of the classification is not considered here. The information presented should, however, provide some basis for making a tentative judgment of the validity of the scheme.

Since success was used as a criterion variable to permit investigation of the question of "optimum organizational structure," the classification was conceived as relational. Absolute criteria of success were not sought.

VERY SUCCESSFUL FIRMS

Firm   **Criteria Used in Evaluation of Success**

1. First production facility of its kind in the area; founded thirty years ago with $39,000; present value of plant now in excess of $200,000,000; new office facilities; entered into retailing of product recently and has developed an expanding chain of successful outlets.
2. One of the "Fortune 500," and holding its position very well.
3. Unit producer of complex machinery; labor force expanding at 5 percent per year; firm's standards on one line used as basis for establishing national standards; recently developed distribution centers to market all of their products; thirty years of continuous growth and recognition in field.
4. Net sales increased 1,000 percent between 1950 and 1955; net profit increased 1,100 percent between 1950 and 1965; labor force increased 700 percent between 1950 and 1965; new home office just constructed; sales now approaching $100,000,000.
5. One of the "Fortune 500" and a leader in its field for years.
6. Relatively small firm with combined ownership and management; specialized production of one line of complex machinery produced on unit basis; noted throughout the industry for engineering development; high cost units custom installed throughout the United States; widely recognized as a leader in its field.
7. Division of one of the "Fortune 100"; second firm in rapidly expanding industry to show a profit.
8. Firm founded in 1959 with a $19,000,000 plant; by 1969 plant value will stand at 40–42 million; one of the first such manufacturers in its field with an estimated lead of two to three years over most competitors.
9. One of the "Fortune 100"; average sales growth of more than 10 percent in past decade; average net profit of 14 percent during past decade.
10. Relatively small manufacturer of complex units; in the past

VERY SUCCESSFUL FIRMS

Firm Criteria Used in Evaluation of Success

five years sales have increased by over 500 percent with an attendent increase in profits; during the past five years two new plants have been constructed; during the past five years a very successful international sales organization has been formed and the company has moved away from dependence on local markets.

11 One of the "Fortune 100"; second largest producer in its field for forty years.

12 One of "Fortune 500"; founded eleven years ago, it was the third firm in a very rapidly expanding industry to show a profit; through acquisitions it has expanded into the area of support systems for its profits and recently acquired a financial firm with assets of several hundred million dollars to finance the very complex marketing of its product.

13 An established firm with an international operation. The fiscal state of this company is used as an informal index of the general economic health of American industry; the firm has recently moved into a new product line, which makes it currently one of the top five manufacturers in two industrial sectors.

14 During the period from 1950 to 1965 this firm, long established in its field, experienced a sales growth of 500 percent while the industry wide growth rate was 300 percent; its relative position in its industrial sector has always been good and has been improving during the past twenty years; sales have been increasing at better than 10 percent a year for the past decade, and profits have been increasing at a greater rate.

15 This is a very large diversified firm which has recently entered the "Fortune 500"; all standard measures of fiscal position show continuous improvement during the decade of the 1960s with the return on invested capital and earnings per share growing proportionately faster than net sales.

16 Established firm; ranks in top ten of large and growing in-

VERY SUCCESSFUL FIRMS

Firm	Criteria Used in Evaluation of Success

dustrial sector; involved in large number of mergers, and plant and product expansions during past decade; relative position in industry improving.

17 Local cooperative; well known for technological innovation; steady growth; success rating not based on any spectacular achievements but on long history of continual improvement of the position of the firm.

18 Division of one of the "Fortune 100"; an undisputed leader in its field.

19 Steady, fifty-year growth to position of leadership in its industry; successfully maintained economic position in industry which has been severely threatened by product lines utilizing different raw materials to provide for the same functions.

20 Unit operation specializing in provision of low-cost product direct to consumer through firm's own sales outlet; one of first manufacturers to create own sales outlet for this kind of product; continual expansion of services to include more area served to the point where it is now the largest manufacturer of this product in the United States.

21 Overall growth rate of 10–12 percent during past decade; firm is competing in industry which has been characterized by regional manufacturers of low-cost batch products; success in developing a national organization is a good indicator of the relative success of the firm's operation.

22 Largest and most successful firm in its industry. One of the "Fortune 100."

23 Very successful national operation which developed initially to serve a local market far removed from raw materials and the remainder of the industry; despite the isolation from materials and the remainder of the industry, its current sales now approach $100,000,000, with a growth rate averaging 8–10 percent for the past decade; recent diversification of lines and products have proved fiscally successful.

24 Largest firm in its field; 17 manufacturing plants; continuous

VERY SUCCESSFUL FIRMS

Firm	Criteria Used in Evaluation of Success

steady growth for thirty years; net profit averaging 9 percent of sales and 50 percent of capital investment.

25 Local small-batch operation; one of a number of local firms which combine to make the area No. 3 in this industry; steady growth characterized by well-managed diversification within the industrial sector.

26 Local firm engaging in relatively new area of manufacturing. Average sales increase in period 1952–59 was 10 percent; average sales increase in period 1960–68 was 20 percent per year.

27 Established leader in industrial area; one of "Fortune 500"; long-term steady growth with continual expansion of plant, markets, and products.

28 Division of one of the "Fortune 100"; largest producer of its line of products.

29 Small-batch producer of complex machinery; division of larger corporation; has experienced sales increases of over 100 percent during several of the past five years.

30 Undisputed leader in the manufacturing of its primary product line; recently engaged in very successful diversification of line involving the introduction of a new product line which could be integrated into the basic manufacturing equipment already utilized.

31 Small continuous-process operation; characterized by steady growth and intensification of its control of a small regional market.

LESS SUCCESSFUL FIRMS

Firm	Criteria Used in Evaluation of Success

32 Large manufacturer; relative position in industry has been slipping for five to ten years; engaged in several unsuccessful attempts to enter new markets.

33 Very small manufacturer of product line not normally pro-

LESS SUCCESSFUL FIRMS

Firm	Criteria Used in Evaluation of Success
	duced in area; modest expansion but production building not owned by firm; production technology has not been changed in forty years, although leaders in the industry are initiating significant changes in production technology.
34	Small producer in industry which has experienced relative decline in the past decade; plant facilities have remained basically the same for forty years with production technology lagging behind industry-wide changes.
35	Division of larger corporation; sales and net profits have fluctuated greatly during past decade.
36	Expanding firm with good growth potential; recent expansions have created organizational chaos which threatens the ability of firm to maintain present markets and to capitalize on recent technological innovations; recently the fiscal position of the firm has varied considerably from year to year.
37	Division of larger corporation; physical plant basically unchanged for the past eighty years; firm's relative position in industry has declined during the past decade.
38	Small firm manufacturing product line not normally found in the area; plant and technology have remained unchanged for thirty years.
39	Erratic sales and profits in an industry experiencing rapid growth during the past decade.
40	Small firm; holding its own financially but not experiencing much growth.
41	Small established firm with little growth during past twenty-five years.
42	Well-known manufacturer of complex machinery; financial position became serious enough to require selling out to a larger corporation; at present, operating as a division, the firm has not recovered financially.
43	Small firm; modest steady growth; limited line of products in rather competitive industry.
44	Modest-size firm with limited product line; experienced

LESS SUCCESSFUL FIRMS

Firm	Criteria Used in Evaluation of Success
	severe financial crisis during 1950's; appears to have recovered from crisis but shows no indication of rapid growth and development.
45	Well-known producer of relatively expensive line of consumer goods; ceased operation in 1967 following a prolonged strike.
46	Division of larger corporation; fiscal crisis in 1950's forced sale of corporation to present parent company; present indicators suggest possibility of significant growth and development, but position is still somewhat difficult to judge.
47	Manufacturer of complex consumer machinery; brand name well-known in highly competitive consumer industry, but fiscal position has been unstable during the past five years; several new lines have not been successful and new competitors have successfully challenged this established firm.
48	Small but very competitive firm; highly specialized product line with very little possibility for growth without diversification; no plans for diversification at present.
49	Firm has experienced two loss years recently in industry characterized by fairly steady growth rate.
50	Small firm; very limited product line; no plans for expansion.
51	Small firm; little growth during past twenty years; no plans for expansion of firm.
52	Limited product line; modest growth; small firm in industry completely dominated by a giant oligarchy.
53	Small family firm; little growth; no plans for expansion.
54	Modest-size firm; secure position in marketing of limited line of products; no plans for expansion of facilities.
55	Medium-size firm in industry where production is increasingly being dominated by larger firms; modest expansion of facilities has not kept pace with industry-wide growth of leaders in the area; relative position in the industry has declined in the past decade.

BIBLIOGRAPHY

Applewhite, Philip B. *Organizational Behavior.* Englewood Cliffs, N. J.: Prentice-Hall, 1965.

Barnard, Chester. *The Functions of the Executive* Cambridge, Mass.: Harvard University Press, 1938.
Blau, Peter M., and Scott, Richard W. *Formal Organizations: A Comparative Approach.* San Francisco: Chandler Publishing Company, 1962.
Blauner, Robert. *Alienation and Freedom: The Factory Worker and His Industry.* Chicago: University of Chicago Press, 1964.
Burke, John G., ed. *The New Technology and Human Values.* Belmont, Calif.: Wadsworth Publishing Company, 1966.
Burns, Tom. *Management in the Electronics Industry—A Study of Eight English Companies.* Edinburgh: Social Science Research Center, University of Edinburgh, 1958.

Caplow, Theodore. "Organizational Size." *Administrative Science Quarterly.* 1 (March, 1957): 484 ff.
———. *Principles of Organization.* New York: Harcourt, Brace & World, 1964.

Chinoy, Ely. *Automobile Workers and the American Dream.* New York: Doubleday & Company, 1955.

Cohen, Morris R., and Nagel, Ernest. "Measurements." In *The Structure of Scientific Thought,* edited by Edward H. Madden. Boston: Houghton Mifflin Company, 1960.

Crozier, Michael. *The Bureaucratic Phenomenon.* Chicago: University of Chicago Press, 1964.

Cyert, Richard M., and March, James G. *A Behavioral Theory of the Firm.* Englewood Cliffs, N. J.: Prentice-Hall, 1963.

Dalton, Melville. *Men Who Manage.* New York: John Wiley & Sons, 1959.

Davis, R. C. *The Influence of the Unit of Supervision and Span of Executive Control on the Economy of Line Organization Structure.* Columbus, Ohio: Bureau of Business Research, Ohio State University, Research Monograph No. 26, 1941.

Dennis, N., Henriques, F., and Slaughter, C. *Coal is Our Life.* London: Eyre & Spottiswoode, 1956.

Dill, William R. "Business Organizations." In *Handbook of Organizations,* edited by James G. March, pp. 1071–1114. Chicago: Rand McNally & Company, 1965.

Dubin, Robert. "Business Behaviorally Viewed." In *Social Science Approaches to Business Behavior,* ed. Chris Argyris et al., Homewood, Ill.: Richard D. Irwin, 1962, p. 25ff.

———. "Supervision and Productivity: Empirical Findings and Theoretical Considerations." In *Leadership and Productivity: Some Facts of Industrial Life,* edited by Robert Dubin et al., pp. 1ff. San Francisco: Chandler Publishing Company, 1965.

———. *Working Union-Management Relations: The Sociology of Industrial Relations.* Englewood Cliffs, N. J.: Prentice-Hall, 1959.

———. *The World of Work: Industrial Society and Human Relations.* Englewood Cliffs, N. J.: Prentice-Hall, 1958.

———. et al. *Leadership and Productivity: Some Facts of Industrial Life.* San Francisco: Chandler Publishing Company, 1965.

Dunlop, John T., ed. *Automation and Technological Change.* Englewood Cliffs, N. J.: Prentice-Hall, 1962.

Durkheim, Émile. *The Division of Labor in Society.* Translated by George Simpson. New York: The Free Press, 1947.

Etzioni, Amitai. *A Comparative Analysis of Complex Organizations.* New York: The Free Press, 1966.
———. *Modern Organizations.* Englewood Cliffs, N. J.: Prentice-Hall, 1964.

Faunce, W. A. "Automation and the Automobile Worker." *Social Problems* 6 (1958):68–78.
———. "Automation in the Automobile Industry: Some Consequences for In-Plant Structure." *American Sociological Review* 23 (1958):401–407.
———. "Automation in the Automobile Industry: Some Consequences for In-Plant and Union-Management Relationships." Microfilmed. Ph.D. dissertation, Wayne State University, Detroit, 1957.
———. "The Automobile Industry: A Case Study in Automation." In *Automation and Society,* edited by H. B. Jacobson and J. S. Roucek, pp. 44–53. New York: Philosophical Library, 1959.
Fensham, Peter J., and Hooper, Douglas. *The Dynamics of a Changing Technology: A Case Study in Textile Manufacturing.* London: Tavistock Publications, 1964.

Galbraith, John K. *The New Industrial State.* Boston: Houghton Mifflin Company, 1967.
Goffman, Irving. *Asylums.* Garden City, New York: Doubleday & Company, 1961.
Gordon, Robert A. "The Executive and the Owner-Entrepreneur." In *Reader in Beaurocracy,* edited by Robert K. Merton et al. New York: The Free Press, 1952.
Gouldner, Alvin W. "Organizational Analysis." In *Sociology Today,* edited by Robert K. Merton, Leonard Broom, and Leonard S. Cottrell. New York: The Free Press, 1954.
———. *Patterns of Industrial Bureaucracy.* New York: The Free Press, 1954.
Graicunas, V. A. "Relationship in Organization." Reprinted in *Papers on the Science of Administration,* edited by Luther Gulick and Lyndall F. Urwick, pp. 181 ff. New York: Institute of Public Administration, Columbia University, 1937.
Grusky, Oscar. "Managerial Succession and Organizational Ef-

fectiveness." *American Journal of Sociology* 69 (July, 1963): 21ff.
Guest, Robert H. *Organizational Change: The Effect of Successful Leadership.* Homewood, Ill.: Richard D. Irwin, 1962.
Gulick, Luther. "Notes on the Theory of Organization." In *Papers on the Science of Public Administration,* edited by Luther Gulick and Lyndall F. Urwick, pp. 1–45. New York: Institute of Public Administration, Columbia University, 1937.

Haberstroh, Chadwick J. "Organization Design and Systems Analysis." In *Handbook of Organizations,* edited by James G. Warren, pp. 1171–1212. Chicago: Rand McNally & Company, 1965.
Hall, Richard H.; Haas, J. Eugene; and Johnson, Norman J. "Organizational Size and Organizational Structure." *American Sociological Review* 32 (December, 1967):903ff.
Harvey, Edward. "Technology and the Structure of Organizations." *American Sociological Review* 33 (April, 1968): 247–259.
Hawley, Amos H. "Population Size and Administration in Institutions of Higher Education." *American Sociological Review* 30 (April, 1965):252–255.
Henry, William E. "Executive Personality," In *The Emergent American Society,* edited by W. Lloyd Warner, pp. 241ff. New Haven: Yale University Press, 1967.

Krupp, Sherman. *Pattern in Organization Analysis: A Critical Examination.* New York: Holt, Rinehart, and Winston, 1961.

Likert, Rensis. *The Human Organization: Its Management and Value.* New York: McGraw-Hill Book Company, 1967.
———. *New Patterns of Management.* New York: McGraw-Hill Book Company, 1961.
Litterer, Joseph A. *Organizations: Structure and Behavior.* New York: John Wiley & Sons, 1963.
Litwak, Eugene. "Models of Bureaucracy Which Permit Conflict." *American Journal of Sociology* 67 (September, 1961):177–184.
———. "Technological Innovation and Theoretical Functions of

Primary Groups and Bureaucratic Structures." *American Journal of Sociology* 73 (January, 1968):468–481.

Madden, Edward H., ed. *The Structure of Scientific Thought.* Boston: Houghton Mifflin Company, 1960.

Mann, F. C., and Hoffman, L. R. *Automation and the Worker: A Study of Social Change in Power Plants.* New York: Holt, Rinehart and Winston, 1960.

———. "Individual and Organizational Correlates of Automation." *Journal of Social Issues* 12, No. 2 (1956):7–17.

March, James G., ed. *Handbook of Organizations.* Chicago: Rand McNally Company, 1965.

Marshall, Alfred. *Principles of Economics,* 9th variorum ed., 2 vols., annotations by C. W. Guillebaud. London: Macmillan & Company, 1961.

Marx, Karl. *Capital: A Critique of Political Economy.* Reprint of Charles H. Kerr and Company's 1906 edition. New York: The Modern Library, n. d.

Meissner, Martin. "Behavioral Adaptations to Industrial Technology." Ph.D. dissertation, University of Oregon, 1964.

Merton, Robert K.; Broom, Leonard; and Cottrell, Leonard S., Jr., eds. *Sociology Today.* New York: The Free Press, 1954.

Meyer, Marshall W. "Automation and Bureaucratic Structure." *American Journal of Sociology* 74 (November, 1968):256–264.

Moore, Wilbur E. *The Impact of Industry.* Englewood Cliffs, N. J.: Prentice-Hall, 1965.

Mosel, James N. "Group Relationships and Participative Management." In *Perspectives in Defense Management.* Washington, D.C.: Industrial College of the Armed Forces, n.d.

Newman, William H. *Administrative Action: The Techniques of Organization and Management.* Englewood Cliffs, N. J.: Prentice-Hall, 1951.

———., and Summer, Charles E., Jr. *The Process of Management: Concepts, Behavior, and Practice.* Englewood Cliffs, N. J.: Prentice-Hall, 1961.

Perrow, Charles. "A Framework for the Comparative Analysis of Organizations." *American Sociological Review* 32 (April, 1967):194–208.

———. "Review of *Industrial Organization: Theory and Practice,* by Joan Woodward." *American Sociological Review* 32 (April, 1967):313–315.

Person, H. S., ed. *Scientific Management in American Industry.* New York: Harper & Brothers, 1929.

Pugh, D. S., et al. "Dimensions of Organization Structure." *Administrative Science Quarterly* 13 (June, 1968):65–105.

Rice, A. K. *Productivity and Social Organization: The Ahmedabad Experiment.* London: Tavistock Publications, 1958.

Rubenstein, Albert H., and Chadwick J. Haberstroh, eds. *Some Theories of Organization.* Rev. ed. Homewood, Ill.: Richard D. Irwin, 1966.

Rushing, William A. "The Effects of Industry Size and Division of Labor on Administration." *Administrative Science Quarterly* 12 (December, 1957):273–295.

———. "Hardness of Material as Related to Division of Labor in Manufacturing Industries." *Administrative Science Quarterly* 13 (September, 1968):229–245.

———. "Organizational Rules and Surveillance: Propositions in Comparative Organizational Analysis." *Administrative Science Quarterly* 10 (March, 1966):423–443.

Sayles, Leonard R. *Personnel: The Human Problems of Management.* Englewood Cliffs, N. J.: Prentice-Hall, 1960.

Schulze, Robert O. "The Role of Economic Dominants in Community Power Structures." *American Sociological Review* 23 (February, 1958):3–9.

Scott, William G. "Organization Theory: an Overview and an Appraisal." *Journal of the Academy of Management* (April 1961):7–26.

Simon, Herbert A. *Administrative Behavior.* 2nd ed. New York: The Free Press, 1957.

———. *Models of Man, Social and Rational.* New York: John Wiley & Sons, 1957.

Smith, Adam. *An Inquiry into the Nature and Causes of the Wealth of Nations.* Edited by Edwin Cannan. New York: The Modern Library, 1937.

Stinchcombe, Arthur L. "Bureaucratic and Craft Administration of Production: A Comparative Study." *Administrative Science Quarterly* 4 (September, 1959):168ff.

Stodgil, R. M., and Shartle, C. L. *Methods in the Study of Administrative Leadership*. Columbus: Bureau of Business Research, Ohio State University, 1955.

Taylor, Frederick W. *Scientific Management*. New York: Harper & Brothers, 1911.

Thompson, Clarence B., ed. *Scientific Management*. Cambridge, Mass.: Harvard University Press, 1914.

Thompson, James D., ed. *Approaches to Organizational Design*. Pittsburgh: University of Pittsburgh Press, 1966.

———. *Organizations in Action*. New York: McGraw-Hill Book Company, 1967.

Thompson, Victor A. *Modern Organization: A General Theory*. New York: Alfred A. Knopf, 1961.

Tönnies, Ferdinand. *Fundamental Concepts of Sociology*. Translated by Charles P. Loomis. New York: American Book Company, 1940.

Trist, E. L., et al. *Organizational Choice: Capabilities of Groups at the Coal Face Under Changing Technologies*. London: Tavistock Publications, 1963.

Udell, John G. "An Empirical Test of Hypotheses Relating to Span of Control." *Administrative Science Quarterly* 12 (December, 1967):420ff.

Udy, Stanley H., Jr. "The Comparative Analysis of Organizations." In *Handbook of Organizations*, edited by James G. March, pp. 678–709. Chicago: Rand McNally & Company, 1965.

———. *Organization of Work: A Comparative Analysis of Production Among Nonindustrial Peoples*. New York: Taplinger Publishing Co., 1959.

Urwick, Lyndall F. *Management of Tomorrow*. London: Nisbet and Co., 1933.

———. "Organization as a Technical Problem." In *Papers on the Science of Administration*, edited by Luther Gulick and Lyndall F. Urwick, pp. 47–88. New York: Institute of Public Administration, Columbia University, 1937.

———. *The Pattern of Management.* Minneapolis: University of Minnesota Press, 1956.

Villers, Raymond. *Dynamic Management in Industry.* Englewood Cliffs, N. J.: Prentice-Hall, 1960.

Walker, Charles R., ed. *Modern Technology and Civilization: An Introduction to Human Problems in the Machine Age.* New York: McGraw-Hill Book Company, 1962.

Warner, W. Lloyd, ed. *The Emergent American Society.* New Haven: Yale University Press, 1967.

———, and Martin, Norman H. *Industrial Man: Businessmen and Business Organizations.* New York: Harper & Row, 1959.

Weber, Max. *The Methodology of the Social Sciences.* Translated by Edward A. Shils and Henry A. Finch. New York: The Free Press, 1949.

———. *The Theory of Social and Economic Organization.* Translated by A. M. Henderson and Talcott Parsons. New York: Oxford University Press, 1947.

Woodward, Joan. *Industrial Organization: Theory and Practice.* London: Oxford University Press, 1965.

———. *Management and Technology,* Problems of Progress in Industry, No. 3. London: Her Majesty's Stationery Office, Department of Scientific and Industrial Research, 1958.

Worthy, James C. *Big Business and Free Men.* New York: Harper & Row, 1959.

———. "Managers, Corporate Structure, and Employee Morale: A Case Study." In *Industrial Man: Businessmen and Business Organizations,* edited by W. Lloyd Warner and Norman H. Martin, pp. 251–258. New York: Harper & Row, 1959.

———. "Organizational Structure and Employee Morale." *American Sociological Review* 15 (April, 1950):169–179.

Zeitlin, Irving. *Ideology and the Development of Sociological Theory.* Englewood Cliffs, N. J.: Prentice-Hall, 1968.

INDEX

administration, "proverb" of, 65
advancement policy, firm size, and 13
  see also promotion policy
American industries, organizational characteristics of, 26–43
authority structure, levels of, 8

British economy, marketplace in, 154
business success, production technology and, 32–33
  see also success; success level

Caplow, Theodore, 14
chief executive, span of control of, 37–38, 75–78, 87–88, 176
Chinoy, Ely, 4
classical analysis, vs. Marxian, 1–22
classical economics
  marketplace in, 125, 153
  organization theory in, 3
classical management theory, Woodward's use of, 46–47

community fairs, economic organization and, 139
community ties
  as independent variable, 17
  success and, 41–42
competition, in English industry, 154
continuous-flow process, 11
control, span of, *see* span of control
cultural variation, institutionalization and, 150–151

decision-making
  centralization of, 8
  individual v. team, 8
Dubin, Robert, xx, 7, 101
Durkheim, Émile, 47, 57

economic dependency, community affairs and, 17, 41–42, 139
  see also local market
economic theory, classical, 3, 125, 153

213

English industry
  competitive position of, 154
  organizational characteristics of, 26–43
Essex studies, *see* South East Essex studies; *see also* Woodward study

firm size, advancement policy and, 13
  see also labor force; large-batch production systems
first-line supervision, span of control of, 38, 68, 76, 145, 177
formal organization
  human decisions and, 6
  human rationality and, 2
  rise to dominance, xvii
  see also organization; production systems and types
"Fortune 500" list, 199
"Fortune 100" list, 199–201
functional analysis, conservatism in, xvi

Gemeinschaft and *Gesellschaft*, 47
Gouldner, Alvin, 4
Graicunas, V. A., 64–65
Guest, Robert H., 4
Gulick, Luther, 64–65

Harvey, Edward, 14n
hierarchy, success and, 37
human-relations theory, in formal organization, 2–3

ideology, formal organization and, xvii
  see also Marxian analysis
independent variables
  interaction of, 86–90
  management level and, 88–89
  in Minneapolis study, 29–36
  in Woodward study, 17–18
industrial organization
  Marxian and classical analyses of, 1–22
  production technology and, xvii, 63

social organization and, 13–14, 124–140
success as aim of, 26–28
technology and, xvii, 63
industry, socioeconomic milieu of, 154–156
institutionalization, culture and, 150–151

labor
  direct-to-indirect ratio, 13
  technology and, 95–122
labor costs
  ownership-management relationships and, 118–121
  production technology and, 107–109
  success level and, 181
labor force
  composition of, 8, 11, 17
  local market dependence and, 131, 136–137
  management level and, 78–79
  management type and, 50–51
  organizational structure and, 13–15, 75–81
  production-nonproduction worker ratio and, 109
  production technology and, 55, 110–111
  promotion policy and, 39, 110, 194
  size of in relation to management type, 50–51
  success level and, 33, 173, 186–187, 192–193
  variables in, 18, 39
large-batch production systems, 11, 16
  greater proportion of in Twin Cities area, 31
  local market dependence of, 135
  in Minneapolis area, 29
  organic management and, 52
  span of control and, 87
  supervisor-manager relationships in, 102
less successful firms, characteristics of, 202–204

liberalism, and formal organization, xvii
line-staff arrangements, 8
local markets
    dependence on, 18–19, 128–140, 153
    labor force and, 130–132
    ownership-management separation and, 196–197
    success level and, 182
    technology and, 133, 137

manager-supervisor ratios, 40, 101–104, 110
management
    classical conception of, 57
    ownership and, 18, 34–35, 118–121
    specialization of, 8
management hierarchy, success level and, 175
management levels, 12
    independent variable and, 88–90
    labor force and, 78–79
    ownership-management separation and, 84–86
    production technology and, 72–74, 89
    span of control and, 91
    success and, 84–86
    technological complexity and, 72–73
management style, 8, 17–18
    business success and, 36–37
    in Marxian analysis, 91
    organization and, 12
    supervisory occupations and, 102
management system
    labor force size and, 51
    organic and mechanistic, 12
    production technology and, 51–52
    success level and, 174
    types of, 45–57
management theory
    classical, xvi, 46–47
    Woodward's use of, 46–47
management types
    factors determining, 48–56

labor force and, 50
ownership and, 49
man-machine relationship, 5
manufacturing industry, local market dependence and, 128–140
market
    local, see local market
    milieu variables and, 127–140
marketplace
    in classical economics, 125, 153
    in Marxian thought, 153
Marshall, Alfred, 3
Martindale, Don, xix
Marx, Karl, 91
    concern with structure and organization, xv
    on technology vs. organization, 3–4
Marxian analysis
    vs. classical, 1–22, 141–158
    labor characteristics and, 121
    marketplace and, 153
    mode of production in, 124–125
    perspective absence in, xv
mass production, 11, 17
    local market dependence and, 130, 134–136
    in Minneapolis area, 29
    organic management and, 52
    primary technology and, 8
    subdivision of work in, 101–102
mass-production firms
    labor costs in, 107–108, 120
    local market dependence and, 130, 134–136
    management level and, 89
    span of control in, 62, 87–88
    supervisor-manager ratios in, 102
    in Twin Cities area, 31
mechanistic systems, and large-batch or mass-production firms, 54
Meissner, Martin, 5
methodology, of Minneapolis study, 166–170
    questionnaire format in, 161–165
Midwest American industries, organizational characteristics of, 26–43

milieu variables, market and, 127–140
Minneapolis firms
 affluent milieu of, 155–156
 criteria for selecting, 19–20, 142–143
 economic situation in, 28
 labor force in, 33
 management-production relationships in, 52–53
 ownership-management relationships in, 50–51
 promotion policy in, 105–107
 success in, 28, 32–33
Minneapolis study
 analysis in, 169–170
 data gathering in, 168–169
 hypothesis of, 21
 independent variables in, 29–36
 methodology and questionnaire in, 161–170
 number and types of firms covered in, 20, 167–168
 plan of analysis in, 21–22
 replication in, 15–22, 60–61, 97–98, 107, 124–125, 142–143, 148–149, 152, 166–168
 span of control in, 66–70
 supervisory-nonsupervisory ratios in, 71–72
 supportive character of, 90–91, 144–146
modernization, primary technology and, 8
Moore, Wilbur, 5

nonmanagerial supervisors, ratio of to managers, 40, 152, 180
nonproduction workers, ratio of to production workers, 39, 98–101, 109, 112–114, 179, 192–193
nonsupervisory personnel, ratio of to supervisory, 38–39, 70–72

operating success
 evaluation of, 198–204
 organizational characteristics and, 10
 see also success; success level
operations, types of, 11
 see also production technology
optimum organizational structure, 198
organic management, 52
organization
 formal, *see* formal organization
 labor force and, 13–15
 management style and, 12
 Marxian and classical theories of, 141–158
 production systems and, 16–17
 shape and form of, 12–13, 17–18, 37–39
 success as aim of, 26–27
 technology and, 10–15
organizational characteristics
 of English and Midwest American industries, 26–43
 operational success and, 10
organizational structure, 60–92
 interaction of independent variables in, 86–90
 labor force and, 75–81
 optimum, 198
 ownership-management separation and, 81–86
 technology and, 63–73
organizational variables, types of, 11
organization-management separation, span of control and, 82–84
 see also ownership-management separation
organization size, mechanical systems and, 50
organization theory
 classical ecomonics and, 3
 new approach to, 157
owner-manager firms, supervisor-manager relations in, 115–118
ownership-management combinations
 labor costs and, 118–121
 organization in, 18, 34–35, 49
 promotion policy and, 118
 supervisory-manager ratios in, 115–118

ownership-management separation, 81–86
  local markets and, 196–197
  span of control in, 188–189
  success and, 174
  technology and, 111–112, 130

personnel, supervisory, *see* supervisory-nonsupervisory personnel ratio
primary technology
  modernization and, 8
  relation of to success, 7
process firms, span of control in, 87
process-manufacturing equipment, capital investment in, 134
process production
  in Minneapolis area, 30
  organic management systems and, 52
  organization and, 17
  types of, 11
production
  Marxian and classical analyses of, 1–22
  scale of, 8
production-nonproduction workers, ratio of, 39, 98–101, 109, 112–114, 179, 192–193
production schedules, predictability of, 128
production systems and types, in Minneapolis area, 8, 29–30
production technology
  business success and, 32
  distribution of, 172
  impact of on industrial organization, xvii
  improved conceptualization and instrumentation in, 149
  industrial organization and, xvii, 63
  labor costs and, 110–111
  labor force and, 55
  local market dependence and, 129–131
  management levels and, 72–74, 89
  management systems and, 51–52
  Marxian analysis of, 124–125
  primacy of, 81
  production-nonproduction worker ratios and, 39, 98–101, 109, 112–114, 179, 192–193
  span of control and, 145-146, 152, 184–185
  success level and, 108, 173
  supervisor-manager ratios in, 103
  supervisory-nonsupervisory ratios in, 71
  Types I–IX, 69–70
  see also technology
promotion policy
  labor force and, 39–41, 110
  of Minneapolis firms, 105–107
  ownership-management relations and, 118
  of southeast Essex firms, 104–105
  success level and, 181, 194
"proverb of administration," 65
psychiatric treatment technologies, 5

questionnaire, format of, 161–165

rationality, human organizations and, 2
Rushing, William A., 14*n*

sales, local markets and, 18–19
sample size, in methodology, 167
self-interest, conflict of, 125
Simon, Herbert A., 65
small-batch production operations, 11, 16, 29
  local markets and, 134, 138
  management level and, 89
  promotion policy in, 105
  span of control in, 87
social life, material factors in, 91
social milieu, 124–140
  variables in, 127–140
  wider aspects of, 151–157
social organization, vs. industrial organization, 13
socioeconomic milieu
  differences in, 154–156

organization theory and, 156–157
solidarity, mechanical and organic, 47–48
South East Essex studies, 6–22
  see also Woodward study
South East Technical College, 6
span of control, 8
  of chief executive, 37–38, 65
  combined ownership-management and, 87–88
  defined, 64
  of first-line supervisor, 38, 68, 76, 145, 177
  labor force and, 75–78
  in large-batch firms, 87
  management level and, 91
  in mass-production firms, 62, 87–88
  of Minneapolis and English firms compared, 67–68
  organization-management separation and, 82–84
  ownership-management separation and, 188
  production technology and, 152
  success level and, 77, 176–177, 184–185
  supervisors and, 12–13
  technology and, 65
  in unit operations, 61–62
Standard Industrial Classification, 167
success
  community ties and, 41–42
  concept of, 26–27
  in English organizations, 27
  evaluation of, 198–204
  hierarchy and, 37, 175
  level of, see success level
  in Minneapolis area, 28
  organizational characteristics of, 10
  primary technology and, 7
  reasons for, 126–127
  see also business success; operating success; success level
successful firms, characteristics of, 199–202

success level
  labor costs and, 181
  labor force and, 186–187, 192–193
  local market dependence and, 134–136
  management hierarchy and, 37, 175
  management-ownership relationship and, 35
  managerial supervisor-manager ratio and, 180
  management system and, 174
  ownership-management separation and, 174, 189–190
  production-nonproduction ratios and, 112–113, 179
  production technology and, 108, 173
  promotion policy and, 181
  span of control and, 77, 176–177, 184–185
  supervisor-manager ratios and, 115–118
  supervisory-nonsupervisory personnel and, 71, 178
  wage-cost allocations and, 40
  see also success
supervisor-manager ratios, success and, 101–104, 110, 115–118
supervisory-nonsupervisory personnel ratios, 12, 70–72, 78, 84, 152, 178
supervisory occupations, management style and, 102

technological determinism, 4
technology
  formal organization and, 5–9, 10–15, 63–73
  industrial organization and, 63
  labor and, 95–122
  local markets and, 133
  major categories of, 11
  Marxism and classical analyses of, 1–22
  ownership-management separation and, 111–112

218

INDEX

see also industrial organization; production technology
Thompson, James D., 5
Tönnies, Ferdinand, 47–48, 57
Twin City Metropolitan Area, industrial success in, 28
see also Minneapolis

Udell, Jon G., 65
unit production operations, 11
  labor costs in, 107
  in Minneapolis study, 29
  organization and, 16
  promotion policy in, 105
  span of control in, 61–62
Ure, Andrew, 3

wage cost allocation, success and, 40
Walker, Charles R., 4
Weber, Max, 15–16
Woodward, Joan, 5, 45, 53, 57, 60, 96, 99, 101, 105, 120, 141–142, 148–149
  first published results (1958), xvi
  use of classical management theory, 46–47
Woodward study
  analysis in, 170
  direct-indirect worker ratio in, 98
  exceptions to, 145–146
  extension of, 15–22, 146–147
  follow-up in, 45
  independent variables in, 17–18
  Marxian analysis and, 97
  nature of, 6–9
  new English industries in, 154
  organization variables in, 42–43
  other variables in, 17–18
  promotion policy in, 104–105
  replication of, 15–22, 60–61, 97–98, 107, 124–125, 142–143, 148–149, 152, 166–168
  small-batch and unit operations in, 61–62
  span of control in, 65, 68–69
  success level vs. production technology in, 32
  supervisor-manager ratio in, 101
  support of, 90–91, 144–145
  variables in, 7, 17–18, 42–43
  wider social milieu and, 151–157
  see also South East Essex study
worker exploitation, in Marxian analysis, 92

Zeitlin, Irving, xviii*n*

DATE DUE			
MAR 8 5			
MAY 30 75			
MAR 2 3 1993			
30 505 JOSTEN'S			